Bill and T[ed] and almost a[t] scored two runs. In the second inning, they scored another two. Disgusted, Bill went to get popcorn. When he returned, he asked, "Anything happen?"

"Truth is," said Ted, "there's good news and bad news. The good news is, one of our guys slid into home plate."

"We got some hits?" Bill asked, looking at the scoreboard.

"Not exactly," said Ted. "The bad news is, he was coming up to bat!"

After the psychiatrist spent an hour with Eve, he said, "My dear woman, I have bad news and good news for you. The bad news is, you have seven different personalities living inside of you."

"That's terrible!" she said. "What's the good news?"

"I've decided to give you a group discount."

The political reporter said to his editor, "The good news is, thanks to the White House press secretary, we got to hear the real *dope* from Washington. The bad news," said the reporter, "is that I mean the *vice president*."

The First
Good News/Bad News
Joke Book

⊘ **SIGNET** (0451)

MORE BIG LAUGHS

☐ **"THE CAT'S GOT YOUR TEETH AGAIN, HERMAN" by Jim Unger.** The hilarious book of cartoons that will have you bursting with laughter.
(160517—$2.50)

☐ **THE JOYS OF YINGLISH by Leo Rosten.** When Yiddish met English, something happened. Something to be treasured. Something to be loved. Here is a book to *nosh* on to your heart's content. "Funny *chummy*, brilliant *schmilliant. The Joys of Yinglish* is a resource, a social document, and an unmitigated joy!"—Norman Lear (173783—$5.99)

☐ **500 GREAT LAWYER JOKES by Jeff Rovin.** Rib-tickling fun inside the courtroom and out. Five hundred hilarious jokes poking fun at everyone involved in the legal system. From lawyers to judges, defendants to plaintiffs—no one is safe when Jeff Rovin enters the courtroom and states its case for laughter. (173872—$3.99)

☐ **500 GREAT BARTENDERS JOKES by Karen Warner.** You'll drink to this! Whether your sense of humor is as spicy as a Bloody Mary, or as dry as a Martini, this raucous collection of laugh-out-loud jokes will have everyone ordering another round of laughter. Cheers! (173880—$3.99)

☐ **GREAT HOAXES, SWINDLES, SCANDALS, CONS, STINGS, AND SCAMS by Joyce Madison.** Features the captivating con men who did their mind-boggling best to prove that honesty is not the best policy. Don't buy the Brooklyn Bridge, buy this book instead. (It'll make you laugh instead of leap!) (173619—$4.99)

Prices slightly higher in Canada

Buy them at your local bookstore or use this convenient coupon for ordering.

NEW AMERICAN LIBRARY
P.O. Box 999 – Dept. #17109
Bergenfield, New Jersey 07621

Please send me the books I have checked above.
I am enclosing $_____ (please add $2.00 to cover postage and handling).
Send check or money order (no cash or C.O.D.'s) or charge by Mastercard or VISA (with a $15.00 minimum). Prices and numbers are subject to change without notice.

Card #_____ Exp. Date _____
Signature_____
Name_____
Address_____
City _____ State _____ Zip Code _____

For faster service when ordering by credit card call **1-800-253-6476**

Allow a minimum of 4-6 weeks for delivery. This offer is subject to change without notice.

The First
Good News/Bad News
Joke Book

■ ■ ■

Jeff Rovin

Ⓢ
A SIGNET BOOK

SIGNET
Published by the Penguin Group
Penguin Books USA Inc., 375 Hudson Street,
New York, New York 10014, U.S.A.
Penguin Books Ltd, 27 Wrights Lane,
London W8 5TZ, England
Penguin Books Australia Ltd, Ringwood,
Victoria, Australia
Penguin Books Canada Ltd, 10 Alcorn Avenue,
Toronto, Ontario, Canada M4V 3B2
Penguin Books (N.Z.) Ltd, 182–190 Wairau Road,
Auckland 10, New Zealand

Penguin Books Ltd, Registered Offices:
Harmondsworth, Middlesex, England

First published by Signet,
an imprint of New American Library,
a division of Penguin Books USA Inc.

First Printing, March, 1993
10 9 8 7 6 5 4 3 2 1
Copyright © Jeff Rovin, 1993
All rights reserved

 REGISTERED TRADEMARK—MARCA REGISTRADA

Printed in the United States of America

Without limiting the rights under copyright reserved above,
no part of this publication may be reproduced, stored in or
introduced into a retrieval system, or transmitted, in any
form, or by any means (electronic, mechanical, photocopying,
recording, or otherwise), without the prior written permission
of both the copyright owner and the above publisher of this
book.

BOOKS ARE AVAILABLE AT QUANTITY DISCOUNTS WHEN USED TO PRO-
MOTE PRODUCTS OR SERVICES. FOR INFORMATION PLEASE WRITE TO
PREMIUM MARKETING DIVISION, PENGUIN BOOKS USA INC., 375 HUD-
SON STREET, NEW YORK, NEW YORK 10014.

If you purchased this book without a cover you should be
aware that this book is stolen property. It was reported as
"unsold and destroyed" to the publisher and neither the author nor the publisher has received any payment for this
"stripped book."

INTRODUCTION

We've got good news and bad news.

The good news is, you're holding the very first good news, bad news joke book, and it's a riot.

The bad news is, you're going to have to install seat belts on all the chairs in your house. Otherwise you'll be rolling on the floor with laughter!

Actually you probably didn't realize that good news, bad news jokes are the *oldest* kind of jokes there are. Why, back in the Stone Age, one of the most popular jokes went like this:

■ ■ ■

"Say, Oggnoggins, I've got good news and bad news."

"What's the good news?" said his caveman friend Uggnuggins.

"Our friend Iggniggins killed a saber-toothed tiger all by himself."

"Really? That's great! So what's the bad news?"

Oggnoggins replied, "The tiger choked to death while eating Iggniggins."

■ ■ ■

It's true: this is the oldest joke known to anthropologists. They found it written on a cave in Lascaux, France.

We hope you enjoy this collection: the good news is, there's another one coming your way. The bad news is, you'll have to wait a few months for it.

So read slowly!

GOOD NEWS
AND BAD NEWS

Loretta came home from her first day at school. "Mom . . . there's good news and bad news. The good news is, Dad gave me two whole dollars for lunch when he dropped me off at school."

"That was very nice of him!"

"Yes," said Loretta. "The bad news is, all the *other* kids ate the sandwiches."

■ ■ ■

"Mr. Mayor," said an aide, "I've got good news and bad news. The good news is, you won the election."

"Phew!" the mayor sighed. "I was worried about that."

"The bad news is, you're the new dogcatcher."

■ ■ ■

Little Billy said to his mom, "Yo, Ma! I've got good news and bad news. The bad news is, the dog walked into a buzz saw and cut off her left side!"

"Oh, my!" said his mother. "Let's get her to the vet quickly!"

"Stay cool," said Billy. "The good news is, she's all right."

■　■　■

"We've got good news about the economy," the President's adviser told him. "There's one group of people that are making a *ton* of money!"

"Glad to hear it," said the Commander-in-Chief.

"Uh . . . the bad news," said the adviser, "is it's all the people who are making 'Going Out of Business' signs."

■　■　■

"Pop," said the farm boy, "the good news is that new scarecrow's working miracles in the field.

"The bad news is, I don't think Grandma can stay out there much longer!"

■　■　■

"Ma, I've got good news for you," said little Roger. "My project worked! I didn't fail chemistry."

"That's wonderful!" his mother said.

"The bad news is, you've got to pay for the lab I blew up."

■ ■ ■

The cabdriver told his wife he had good news and bad news.

"The good news is that we've got money to burn. The bad news," he said, "is it's cheaper than burning gas."

■ ■ ■

The publisher told the writer, "There's good news and bad news. The bad news is, I was very excited by your last novel.

"The good news," said the publisher, "is that's because it *was*."

■ ■ ■

The pilot got on the intercom.

"Uh . . . ladies and gentleman, I've got some bad news for you: the aircraft's been struck by lightning.

"But I've also got some good news: we'll still be reaching the airport on time.

"The bad news is, the cabin, wings, and tail section will be arriving separately."

■ ■ ■

"Martha," said the stable owner, "I've got good news! The cat's been declawed!

"The bad news is, the horse whose butt they're stuck in kicked the rest of kitty into the next county."

■ ■ ■

The lawyer approached his client. "Bob, the good news is, the judge let you off with a small fine for running that little old lady off the road.

"The bad news is, her name is Mrs. Corleone."

■ ■ ■

"Ms. Kidd," said her boss, "the bad news is, the orange juice company fired you.

"The good news is, at least you won't have to concentrate anymore."

■ ■ ■

The newscaster said, "The bad news is that the President is asking the Congress to raise taxes again.

"But there's good news," she continued. "The increase will only affect people who are earning any income."

■ ■ ■

The two college girls were staring at a hunky young guy.

"The good news," said one, "is I hear he got his good looks from his father."

"True," said the other. "The bad news is, his father's a plastic surgeon."

■ ■ ■

When Linda, an aspiring actress, came home from an audition, she said to her mother, "What a day I had! The good news is, a man said, 'Stick with me, kid, and you'll go places!'"

"How nice!" her mother said.

"Yes, but the bad news is, he was a cabdriver."

■ ■ ■

The ski instructor said to his ambitious student, "I've got good news, Jess. Frankly I've never seen anyone who's better at ski jumping.

"The bad news is, jumping over your skis isn't an Olympic event!"

■ ■ ■

Greg was saying to his friend, "The good news is, just this morning I finally found myself enjoying my dad's company.

"The bad news is, this afternoon he fired me."

Sam walked over to his friend Mike.

"Hey, Mike, did you ask Megan out last night?"

"Yes," said Mike, "and the good news is that we finally went out.

"The bad news is, I found out there's nothing more expensive than a girl who's free for the evening."

■ ■ ■

Cindy stormed into the house after her first date and said to her younger sister, "The good news is, I found out what necking is.

"The bad news is, whoever named it didn't know much about anatomy!"

■ ■ ■

The two diners were discussing their meal.

"The good news," said one, "was that they let me put the filet mignon on my charge card.

"The bad news was, it fit!"

■ ■ ■

Doreen said to Michael, "The good news is, there's still that familiar gleam in my dad's eye when he wakes up each morning.

"The bad news is, he never manages to get the toothpaste in his *mouth*."

■ ■ ■

In one state a while back, they said, "The good news is, Governor Lapetomain is leaving the state!

"The bad news is, he's running for President!"

■ ■ ■

"The good news," said the political analyst to Governor Lapetomain, "is that many voters feel you're a pain in the neck."

"That's the *good* news?" screamed the governor.

"Yes, ma'am," said the analyst. "The bad news is, other people have a much lower opinion of you."

■ ■ ■

If you think about it, though, the good news is, the governor achieved her goals, because she always wanted to be governor in the worst way.

The bad news is, she succeeded.

■ ■ ■

"The good news," Mrs. Farrell told her friend, "is that my husband helps with the housework.

"The bad news is, when he lifts his legs, I'm still the one pushing the vacuum under them."

■ ■ ■

The economist said, "The good news is, we're no longer creeping into a depression.

"The bad news is, we're jogging."

■ ■ ■

"The good news," the politician's aide confided to a friend, "is that my boss is a leader of men.

"The bad news is he's also a follower of women."

■ ■ ■

"The good news," Marie said of her dentist, "is that when he tells you it won't hurt, it doesn't.

"The bad news is, he means *him*."

■ ■ ■

"The bad news," the dentist said to Ms. Blyth, "is that you have a new cavity.

"The good news is, the gold in your old fillings has quadrupled in value."

■ ■ ■

The old man said to his dentist, "The good news is, my false teeth fit just fine.

"The bad news is, I'm talking about in the glass, *not* in my mouth."

■ ■ ■

"The good news," said the young man, "is that I'm putting enough money into the bank to take care of my future.

"The bad news is, I'm broke *today!*"

■ ■ ■

"The bad news," Mr. Scott told the police, "is that my car was stolen.

"The good news is, my boss was in it."

■ ■ ■

"The bad news," said the news commentator, "is that Congress just voted itself a pay raise.

"The good news is, the government's so broke the checks will bounce."

■ ■ ■

"The bad news," the young woman told her friend, "is that my new guy's a cad.

"The good news is, so's his limo."

■ ■ ■

Ms. Gallo said to Ms. Mellis, "The good news is, I'm doing great on my garlic diet.

"The bad news is, you don't really lose any weight, you just look skinnier because people stand farther away."

■ ■ ■

Ryan was saying of his teacher, "The good news is, Mr. Pratt says what he thinks.

"The bad news is, most of the time he's speechless."

■ ■ ■

Ryan continued, "The good news is, Mr. Pratt went to a mind reader.

"The bad news is, she felt guilty charging him more than half price."

■ ■ ■

Mr. Dummo said to his wife, "The bad news is, we've got a lot of flies in the house.

"The good news is, I opened all the windows and screens to let them out."

■ ■ ■

"Good news!" said the gossip columnist. "People in Hollywood have found a way to add years to their lives!

"The bad news," the columnist continued, "is that it's by telling the truth about their age."

■ ■ ■

The political reporter said to his editor, "The good news is, thanks to the White House press secretary, we got to hear the real dope from Washington.

"The bad news," said the reporter, "is that I mean the Vice-President."

■ ■ ■

The doctor thought hard to figure out a way to tell his patient that she had to lose weight.

"The good news," said the doctor, "is that you're a master when it comes to body language.

"The bad news," he said, "is that your vocabulary is just a *bit* too large."

■ ■ ■

John met Karen at the mall. "How's your new car?" he asked.

"Well," she said, "there's good news and bad news. The good news is, there are lots of options.

"The bad news is, our options are towing it, abandoning it, or trading it in for a car that *works*!"

∎ ∎ ∎

Karen finally got fed up and took the car in to be serviced.

"There's good news and bad news," said the mechanic. "The good news is, there's one part of your car that isn't making any noise at all.

"The bad news is, it's the horn."

∎ ∎ ∎

The poor young man stood before the judge.

"Your Honor," said the defendant, "there's good news and bad news. The good news is, I didn't steal the money from the bank.

"The bad news is, as soon as I told my lawyer, she dropped me."

∎ ∎ ∎

At the presidential debate, candidate Smith said, "There's good news and bad news about my opponent Jones. The good news is, he says he's got electability.

"The bad news is, he doesn't understand that that should be two words."

■ ■ ■

Mike and Harleigh were walking to school one day.

"You know what's funny? The good news is, my parents said that going to school would be the happiest time of life.

"The bad news is, they meant *their* lives."

■ ■ ■

"The good news," said the Washington, D.C., minister, "is that Congress is still permitted to open each session with a prayer.

"The bad news is, it doesn't seem to do a bit of good!"

■ ■ ■

The senator didn't agree that things were so bad in Congress.

"The good news," he told the voters at a rally, "is that in Congress, we don't pass the buck anymore."

Someone in the audience yelled, "The bad news is, you keep it!"

■ ■ ■

"You think inflation is bad?" John said to Beryl. "Let me tell you some good news: I just bought a used car for $8,000."

"That's great!" said John.

"Sure," said Beryl. "But the bad news is, it only cost $6,000 when it was new!"

■ ■ ■

Mrs. Fiftal said to Mrs. McHare, "The good news is, my doctor's handwriting is very legible.

"The bad news," she went on, "is that I can read his bill."

■ ■ ■

A week after being fired, Mr. Taylor said to his friend, "The good news is, losing my job has brought my family and me closer together.

"The bad news is, it's because we had to move to a smaller apartment."

■ ■ ■

Willie showed up at school all battered and bruised.

"What happened?" a friend asked.

"Good news and bad news," Willie said. "The good news is, I threw a party last night."

"Say, that sounds like fun!"

Willie shook his head. "The bad news is, the party in question didn't *want* to be thrown."

■ ■ ■

Tina and Tiffany were sitting in the cafeteria when the handsome new student entered and sat down nearby.

"Get a load of him!" said Tina.

"He's a hunk," agreed Tiffany, "but there's good news and bad news about him. The good news is, he really makes heads turn."

"So what's the bad news?" asked Tina.

"The bad news," said Tina, looking away as he stuffed half a sandwich in his mouth, "is that when he eats, he makes stomachs turn."

■ ■ ■

At the end of the day, the teacher said to little Jill, "I have bad news and good news for you. The bad news is, you just weren't yourself today."

"I know," said Jill.

"The good news is, it's a big improvement!"

■ ■ ■

The priest said to the woman, "Mrs. Rachlin—where is your husband? I didn't see him in church today."

"Well," she replied, "I've got good news and bad news. The good news is, he bowed his head this morning, just like the rest of us.

"The bad news is, it was over a golf ball."

■ ■ ■

When Tom got home, he said to his brother Steve, "Guess what? A great-looking young woman approached me in the street today."

"What happened?" asked Steve.

"I have good news and bad news about that," Tom replied. "The good news was, she walked up and said, 'How are you, you handsome devil?'

"The bad news was, she only stopped to ask directions to the eye doctor's office."

■ ■ ■

The scientist said to the farmer, "Sir, I've developed a new breed of chicken that will save you a fortune. You don't have to give it feed."

"No feed?" said the farmer. "That *will* save me a lot. What does it eat?"

"I'll tell you," said the scientist, "but there's good news and bad news. The good news is, it eats grass, leaves, flowers—anything from the yard.

"The bad news is, it only lays eggplants."

■ ■ ■

The farmer said to the scientist, "Y'know, I have good news and bad news for *you*. The good news is, you're a good egg.

"The bad news is, you know where eggs come from!"

■ ■ ■

Jake said to his friend Lou, "So, how has life been since you stopped working for a big company and opened your own business?"

"I've discovered that there's good news and bad news about what I did. The good news is that I'm no longer an unknown failure.

"The bad news," he said glumly, "is that now I'm a *known* failure."

■ ■ ■

After reviewing the young man's job performance, his boss said, "Jenkins, I have good news and bad news. The good news is, you have no equals."

"Great!"

The boss scowled. "The bad news is, everyone is your superior!"

■ ■ ■

Mr. Watt said to Mr. Edison, "Now that my son has gotten married, I've told him that there's good news and bad news about having children.

"The good news is that they're a comfort to you in your old age.

"The bad news is, they help you reach it a whole lot faster!"

■ ■ ■

The newspaper columnist gave a lecture at a local college, and a student approached her as she was leaving.

"I wasn't there for your talk," the student began, "but I have good news and bad news. The good news is, I never miss your column.

"The bad news is, I never read it—which is why I don't miss it."

■ ■ ■

After paying to see a celebrated movie star's debut on the Broadway stage, Donato waited by the stage door until the star came out.

When she emerged, Donato said, "I just wanted to say that after seeing your performance, I have good news and bad news. The good news is, I think the world of you!"

"Thank you," said the snotty star.

"The bad news is, do you have *any* idea what rotten shape the world is in?"

■ ■ ■

"I'll say this about acting," said the aspiring young star, "there's good news and bad news about this profession.

"The good news is, one day you can be delivering a magnificent soliloquy written by Shakespeare.

"The bad news is, the next day you can be delivering a pizza by Domino's."

■ ■ ■

Then there was the playwright who found out there was bad news, good news, and bad news about his show's opening night.

The bad news is that there was a lot of booing. The good news is that there was scattered applause. The bad news is that they were clapping for the people who were booing!

■ ■ ■

"Ma!" the aspiring young actress screamed into the phone, "there's good news and bad news!"

"Tell me the good news first!" said the girl's mother.

"Okay. The good news is, I got to say my first words in a Broadway theater!"

"Congratulations! What were they?"

"That's the bad news: they were, 'Would you like to buy a program, ma'am?' "

■ ■ ■

"There's bad news and good news," the phone-company representative told the customer whose bill was way overdue.

"The bad news is, we've got to disconnect your phone. But the good news is, at least none of your other creditors will be able to call you."

■ ■ ■

When her friend Melanie returned to work after a long illness, Hillary said to her, "How do you feel?"

"To tell you the truth, there's good news and bad news," Melanie replied. "The good news is, my doctor got me back on my feet again.

"The bad news is, it's because I had to sell my car to pay his bill."

■ ■ ■

The sulking woman said to her sports-nut husband, "You dork! You love sports more than you love me!"

The husband said, "Honey, all I've got to say is that there's bad news and good news. The bad news is that I *do* love baseball more than I love you—but the good news is, I love you more than football!"

■ ■ ■

The heavyset man said to his doctor, "Before you lecture me about my health, I want you to know there's good news and bad news.

"The good news is, I'm into weight lifting."

"That's very good," said the doctor.

"The bad news," said the man, "is for me, that means just getting out of a chair."

■ ■ ■

The doctor examined the heavyset patient, then said, "I have good news and bad news regarding your health."

"Let me have the bad news first," said the man.

"Okay. The bad news is, I'm recommending a triple bypass."

The patient went pale.

"As for the good news," the doctor continued, "all that means right now is that I want you to bypass cake, cookies, and candy."

■ ■ ■

Mr. LaMay and Mr. LaJoie had adjoining beds in a hospital room.

"I hear there's good news and bad news

about this hospital," said Mr. LaMay. "The good news is, you're actually allowed to kiss that beautiful Nurse LaFond."

"Really?" said Mr. LaJoie.

"Really. The bad news is, she only comes in to put the thermometer in your mouth."

■ ■ ■

Jenny was talking to a neighbor about the grumpy old man who lived across the street from them.

"You know, I think there's good news and bad news about old Mr. Michaelson," she said. "The good news is that he's got a *lot* of kindness in him.

"The bad news is, it's because he never lets any of it out."

■ ■ ■

Dennis was telling the new student about their teacher, Mr. Wilson.

"There's good news and bad news about him," said the lad. "The good news is, he makes his students *very* happy during the year.

"The bad news is, that only happens when he's home sick."

■ ■ ■

At the annual doctors and nurses dance at the hospital, Marlene said to Anna, "Do you see Dr. Gish over there? The surgeon sitting by himself?"

"Yes."

"Let me tell you the good news about him—he's the best dancer in the hospital."

"So why's he sitting by himself?"

"That's the bad news: whenever he says, 'May I cut in?' the women run the other way."

■ ■ ■

Mrs. Miller to her friend, "I go to a wonderful family doctor. The good news is, he treats mine—

"The bad news is, I support his."

■ ■ ■

The cub scout was late for the den meeting.

"Billy, what took you so long?" Mr. Wallace asked.

"Sir, there's good news and bad news about that. The good news is, I was helping an old lady across the street."

"I see. That's very commendable of you. And what's the bad news?"

Billy replied, "She didn't want to go."

■ ■ ■

SOME TAXING
GOOD NEWS/BAD NEWS ...

Mr. Gideon was talking to his friend at the ritzy country club.

"Is my accountant any good?" Mr. Gideon was saying. "My dear fellow, let me put it this way. There's good news and bad news about him.

"The good news is, there's no one better when it comes to handling numbers.

"The bad news is, the government has him wearing one for the next seven years."

■ ■ ■

Mr. Gideon added, "He's much better than the accountant I had before, Mr. Bigelow.

"The good news about Bigelow is that he'll make you a tidy fortune if you can get to him.

"The bad news is, it's because there's a huge reward out for information leading to his arrest."

■ ■ ■

Mr. Gideon concluded, "There's good news and bad news about my latest accountant as well.

"The good news is, he saves me a lot of money on my income tax. A fortune, in fact.

"The bad news is, everything I save I pay to him!"

■　■　■

Turns out Mr. Gideon's accountant wasn't all that great.

"I have good news and bad news," she said, after going over all his records. "The good news is, I can keep you from going broke next year.

"The bad news is, you can only do it by declaring bankruptcy *this* year."

■　■　■

Mad Marvin said to his friend, "I got some good news and bad news today.

"The good news is, someone told me I had a really impressive collection of Elvis, Buddy Holly, and Chuck Berry records.

"The bad news is, those weren't the records the IRS auditor wanted to see."

■　■　■

Mr. Pettibone was always complaining to his landlord, Mr. Morgan, who finally had enough.

After sending up an exterminator, Mr. Morgan called Mr. Pettibone at work and said, "Sir—I've got good news and bad news for you.

"The good news is, the cockroaches in your apartment are gone.

"The bad news is, I'm evicting you for keeping pets."

■ ■ ■

Marco was an amazing young man: after working for years and years, he finally trained his dog to speak and fulfilled his lifelong dream of becoming part of a circus.

Unfortunately the day after he joined, there was good news and bad news. The good news was that the dog was a hit.

The bad news was, he told Marco to get lost.

■ ■ ■

Then there was the theater critic who wrote a short review of a play that consisted only of good news and bad news.

"The good news," she said, "is that the scenery is absolutely stunning.

"The bad news," she went on, "is that the actors get in front of it."

The critic really *was* a toughie: she went to see a play the next night and wrote an equally short review.

"The good news," she wrote, "is that there's just one thing wrong with the play.

"The bad news," she continued, "is that what's wrong is the fact that the seats face the stage."

■ ■ ■

The foreign-exchange student came to live with an American family and wrote back home, "My dear parents: I find that there's bad news and good news about America, especially about TV.

"The bad news is, the programs are terrible.

"The good news is, I'm learning a lot thanks to TV. Whenever it's on, I go and read a book."

■ ■ ■

The young man said to his new coworker, "I've got some bad news and some good news.

"The bad news is the boss wants to see you so she can speak her mind.

"The good news is, that won't take very long."

■ ■ ■

Mrs. Johnson said to her friend, "I made a special deal with the grocer in town—a good news, bad news deal."

"Oh?" said the friend. "What kind of deal is that?"

"The good news is, the grocer lets me pay him every *two* weeks.

"The bad news is, we can't afford groceries with what my husband earns in *one* week."

■ ■ ■

After moving into a new town, Mrs. Merritt came home and told her husband, "I have good news and bad news about this Dr. Saperstein I went to.

"The good news is, he showed a lot of concern—got right down to business and asked me what I have."

"That's encouraging," said Mr. Merritt

"The bad news is, he meant my health coverage."

■ ■ ■

The rookie police officer walked up to the desk sergeant.

"How was your first day on the beat?" the sergeant asked.

"There's good news and bad news, sir."

"Let me have the good news first."

"Well, sir—I handed out three hundred parking tickets."

"Excellent," said the sergeant. "What's the bad news?"

"Sir," said the rookie, "I have *no* idea what a drive-in movie theater is."

■ ■ ■

Then there was the travel agent who told customers, "I have a good news trip and a bad news trip for you.

"The good news trip is, if you go to Las Vegas, you can get away from it all.

"The bad news is, if you go there, they can get it all away from you."

■ ■ ■

There's more good news, bad news about Las Vegas. The good news is, it's possible to leave the city with a small fortune. The bad news is, to do that you have to start with a large fortune.

■ ■ ■

The inventor told the convention of inventors, "I've come up with the most remarkable machine ever made. However, there's good news and bad news.

"The good news is, my amazing invention does the work of fifty men."

"So what could the bad news be?" asked one of the inventors.

"The bad news is, it takes seventy men to run it."

■ ■ ■

The President's economic adviser cleared his throat and said to the reporters at the White House, "Ladies and gentlemen—I have good news and bad news about the economy.

"The good news is, a dollar goes farther than ever before.

"The bad news is, that's because you can carry one around for days without ever finding anything to buy with it."

■ ■ ■

The economist also said, "I have more good news: research shows that people are finding it easier than ever to balance their checkbooks.

"The bad news is, that's because they're broke."

■ ■ ■

The lawyer said to his client, "I have good news and bad news about your case.

"The good news is, I should be done with it in about three weeks.

"The bad news is, you won't be done with it for about four-to-six years."

■ ■ ■

"Mr. President," said the economic adviser, "I have good news and bad news about the upcoming election.

"The good news is, your opponent has decided not to attack our economic policies.

"The bad news is, we don't have any."

■ ■ ■

After the President returned from a trip abroad, the press asked him how he felt about foreign aid.

"Well, the good news is that I'm all for it.

"The bad news is, I can't find any country that'll give it to us."

■ ■ ■

"I have good news for you!" the aspiring actor told his landlord. "I just got a part in a play! One day you'll be able to tell prospective tenants that I, Samuel Lawrence, once lived here!"

"I have bad news for you," the landlord told Sam. "If you don't pay last month's rent, that day will be tomorrow."

■ ■ ■

The psychiatrist said to his patient, "I have good news and bad news. The good news is, you don't have an inferiority complex."

"Thank goodness!" said the patient. "What's the bad news?"

"The bad news," said the analyst, "is that you really *are* inferior!"

■ ■ ■

Mrs. Olson said to Mrs. Joseph, "My doctor put me on a new diet that's guaranteed to work."

"Really? Tell me about it!"

"Well," said Mrs. Olson, "there's good news and bad news. The good news is, it's a pasta diet."

"Sounds yummy!" said Mrs. Joseph.

"It sure does. The bad news is, in order for it to work you've got to walk pasta bakery, pasta ice-cream shop, pasta fast-food restaurants. . . ."

■ ■ ■

"Yes," the lad said to a friend, "my dad was a special man. However, it would be fair to say that there was good news and bad news where his professional activities were concerned.

"The good news was, Dad carved quite a career for himself in business.

"The bad news was, he did it by becoming a chiseler."

■ ■ ■

Farmer McDonald's mother-in-law was kicked in the head by a mule and ended up in the hospital. While the farmer was visiting the unconscious woman a nurse poked her head in the door.

"Mr. McDonald," she said, "I have good news and bad news for you."

"Lemme have it," he said.

"The good news is, the lobby is full of people who would like to come in."

"That's mighty neighborly of them."

The nurse winced. "The bad news is, they want to talk to you about buying the mule."

■ ■ ■

The once-glamorous movie actress was being interviewed, and said there was good news and bad news about her legendary beauty.

"The good news is that my beauty comes from within.

"The bad news," she continued, "is that it comes from within makeup tubes, jars, and bottles."

■ ■ ■

SOME GOOD NEWS/BAD NEWS ON THE JOB

Disgruntled, Sarah went in to see her boss.

"Mr. Tobin," she said, "I want a raise. Now."

Tobin looked at her. "Why?"

"Well—I have good news and bad news. The good news is, there are three companies that would love to get their hands on me."

"And what's the bad news?" Tobin asked.

Sarah replied, "The companies are the phone, electric, and water."

■ ■ ■

When Sarah didn't get her raise, she complained to a friend, "There's good news and bad news about my boss.

"The good news is, he worked his way to the top even though he lacked certain advantages his rivals had.

"The bad news is, those advantages are tact, talent, and brains."

■ ■ ■

But Sarah didn't let the setback get her down.

"The good news about my boss," she said, "is that you can't help but like him.

"The bad news is, if you don't, you're fired."

■ ■ ■

There's a moral to this story: the good news is, before you ask for a raise, get on your boss's good side.

The bad news is, the best way to get there is by not asking for a raise.

■ ■ ■

The computer expert told his boss, Ms. Smythe, that there was good news and bad news: the good news was that he had designed a great new system for the office, one that would replace all the deadbeats in the company.

The bad news was, it wouldn't tremble when she yelled at it.

■ ■ ■

Ms. Smythe was impressed, and the first thing she did was call young, expendable Mohalley into the office.

"I have bad news and good news," she told him. "The bad news is, I'm going to have to fire you.

"The good news is, I can't stand to see a grown man cry, so—I'm taking off my glasses."

■ ■ ■

Mohalley protested. "Ma'am," he said, "I don't understand. I thought you liked me!"

Ms. Smythe said, "Well, there's good news and bad news. The good news is, you *are* like a son to me.

"The bad news is, my son is an obnoxious, lazy pain in the butt!"

As soon as Iovino sat down to dinner in his favorite restaurant, the small band started playing.

"Waiter," Iovino said, motioning him over, "I have good news and bad news for you.

"The good news is, I have a request for the band.

"The bad news is, it's that they play checkers until I'm through dining."

■ ■ ■

The boy said to his great-great-grandfather, "Is it *really* tougher to do things when you get old?"

The old man huffed. "My boy," he said, "let me put it to you this way. The good news is I can *still* bend down and tie my shoelace.

"The bad news is, I have to try to think of other things to do while I'm down there."

■ ■ ■

"Is there *anything* good about being old?" the boy asked.

"I'll tell you," said his great-great-grandfather. "There's more good news and bad news. The good news is, after having lived in New York all my life, I *really* know my way around.

"The bad news is, I don't feel like going."

■ ■ ■

Little Billy and Little Willy were sitting in front of the TV, watching a Red Sox game, when Billy said, "Boy, I had a strange dream last night."

"Was it a good dream or a bad dream?" Willy asked.

"There were good parts and bad parts," said Billy. "The good part was, I was walking down the street wearing nothing but a base-ball cap."

"Hold on—that's the *good* part? Then what was the bad part?"

Billy replied, "It was a Yankees cap."

■ ■ ■

After the psychiatrist spent an hour with Eve, he said, "My dear woman, I have bad news and good news for you.

BAD NEWS/GOOD NEWS
ABOUT MONEY . . .

The bad news is, money can't buy you happiness.

The good news is . . .

. . . it can buy a yacht so you can sail up *real* close to it.

. . . it can help you look for it in more places.

. . . it lets you rent it for a while.

. . . it makes being unhappy more pleasant. . . .

"The bad news is, you have seven different personalities living inside of you."

"That's terrible!" she said. "What's the good news?"

He said, "I've decided to give you a group discount."

■ ■ ■

The wise man says: the good news is that you'll get ahead if you look out for number one. The bad news is, if you're not careful you may step in number two.

■ ■ ■

Then there was the news anchor person who broke into the TV show with this bulletin: "The bad news is, a boat carrying many senators and representatives has capsized in the Atlantic. At least half of Congress has been lost.

"The good news is, the country has been saved."

■ ■ ■

The young woman had just passed the bar and was saying to a friend, "Now that I'm a lawyer, I have good news behind me and bad news ahead.

"The good news is that I wouldn't have made it without my parents. They lent me $20,000 to go through law school."

"And you *made* it," said her friend, "so how can there be bad news ahead? I hear you've even got your first case lined up."

"That's true," said the woman. "The bad news is, it's against my parents. They're suing me for the money."

■ ■ ■

Then there was a different young attorney who had bad news and good news for *his* parents. The bad news was that he didn't graduate. The good news was that he settled out of class.

■ ■ ■

The good news is that they've opened a library dedicated to President Bush.

The bad news is, there are no books to read—only lips.

■ ■ ■

Then there was the accountant who pointed out, "The good news is, it pays to be an American 364 days a year.

"The bad news is, *you* pay to be an American on April 15th."

■ ■ ■

The former marine said to his new wife, "The good news, my darling, is that your cooking makes me feel young again.

"The bad news is, I feel like I'm back in boot camp."

■ ■ ■

The good news is, there's a renewed "Buy American" attitude sweeping the land.

The bad news is, only the Japanese can afford to.

■ ■ ■

During the presidential primaries, there's always good news and bad news.

The good news is, the field of candidates narrows as the season progresses.

The bad news is, so do their minds.

■ ■ ■

As the election nears, in fact, there's good news and bad news about the candidates.

The good news is, they're increasingly concerned about unemployment.

The bad news is, the concern is for their own.

■ ■ ■

The man was celebrating his one hundredth birthday and said there was bad news and good news about reaching that milestone.

"The bad news is, I don't get around much these days.

"The good news is, I'm walking *much* better than I was a century ago."

■ ■ ■

The United Nations voted to elect the island of Samoa as a member. That was the good news. The bad news was that they wouldn't let its leader address the ambassa-dors: seems there's no Samoa king allowed.

■ ■ ■

The shepherd said to his friend, "You know what I call it when my sheep are quiet?"

"Nope."

"Good news. And you know what I call it when they make too much noise?"

"Nope."

The shepherd said, "*Baaaaa*-d news."

■ ■ ■

The heavyset man went to the Weight Los-ers Club, and when he came home, he told his wife that there was good news and bad news.

"The good news," he said, "is that I feel like a new man.

"The bad news is, the new guy wants a cupcake."

■ ■ ■

SUPERHERO GOOD NEWS/BAD NEWS . . .

The commissioner said, "Batman—I've got good news and bad news for you.

"The good news is, we caught the Cat-woman while she was eating a bird.

"The bad news is, the bird was Robin."

■ ■ ■

The Incredible Hulk was walking down the street when he saw Wonder Woman shooting some hoops on a basketball court. Thundering over, he stole the ball and engaged her in a hard-fought game of one-on-one.

When they were finished, Wonder Woman said, "Hulk—I've got some good news and bad news about the game.

"The good news is, you gave me quite a workout.

"The bad news is, I was playing with Invisible Girl before you came, and you squashed her flat."

■ ■ ■

The people of Smallville wanted to honor Krypto, the heroic dog owned by Superboy.

"The good news," the mayor told the

Boy of Steel, "is that the dinner and dance are going ahead as scheduled. The bad news is, you can't come."

"Why not?" asked Superboy.

"Because the bad news is that the organizers misunderstood when I said I wanted the motif in the hall to be 'Krypto night.' "

... AND SOME MONSTER GOOD NEWS/BAD NEWS

After a brief nap, Dracula rose from his coffin and found a young man strolling in the woods.

As Dracula was about to bite his neck the man said, "Count—I've got good news and bad news.

"The good news is, I don't have any garlic or crosses with me.

"The bad news is, you are waking up during a *very* short solar eclipse!"

■ ■ ■

Good news: the Statue of Liberty getting a complete makeover and looking better than ever.

Bad news: King Kong coming to town 'cause he heard she's a real babe!

■ ■ ■

The police chief of an Eastern European village came to see the mayor.

"I've got good news and bad news," he said. "The good news is that the entire colony of werewolves has been destroyed."

"Splendid!" said the mayor. "So what could be bad?"

"Well, sir, now there's this *huge* cloud of fleas heading our way. . . ."

■ ■ ■

The general ran in to see the Japanese prime minister.

"Sir," said the officer, "I have bad news and good news. The bad news is that Rodan has flown into Tokyo and kidnapped your wife."

"Hmmm," said the prime minister, "that *is* bad news. What's the good news?"

"Well, sir, think of the frequent-flier miles!"

... AND SOME DINOSAUR GOOD NEWS/BAD NEWS

Good news when you spot a giant meat-eater: Tyrannosaurus ignores.

Bad news when you spot a giant meat-eater: Tyrannosaurus wrecks.

■ ■ ■

The dumb brontosaurus sidled up to the dumb stegosaurus, who was munching on plants by the lake.

"What's happening with that volcano near the ocean?" the stegosaurus asked.

"I've got bad news and good news about that. The bad news is, it's erupted and there's a *lot* of lava rolling toward us."

"Yikes! We'd better run!"

"Relax. The good news is, there's a herd of hungry allosauruses headed our way, and they'll get us first."

When Jenny returned home, her sister asked how her date went with the race-car driver.

"There's good news and bad news about that," Jenny said. "The good news is, he was very attentive.

"The bad news is, every time I asked him to pass the salt or ketchup, he asked, 'How fast is it going?' "

■ ■ ■

The police chief said to the mayor, "I've got the report on motor-vehicle accidents, and there's bad news and good news.

"The bad news is, a person is run over every hour in our state."

"That's terrible!" said the mayor. "What's the good news?"

"Fortunately we've convinced the poor clod not to come outside anymore."

■ ■ ■

Jessica returned from Niagara Falls and was telling a coworker about her honeymoon.

"I'll bet it was lovely," the coworker said.

"It was," said the newlywed, "though there was good news and bad news. The good news was that my husband's mouth dropped when he saw the falls.

"The bad news is, it's because it fell off the boat with the rest of him."

■ ■ ■

Then there was the zoologist who pointed out that there's good news and bad news about elephants. The good news is, an elephant never forgets.

The bad news is, it has nothing to remember.

The boy ran into the house.

"Ma! I was having a picnic at the pond with Dad and—well, there's bad news and good news."

"What is it?"

"The bad news is, Dad's croaking!"

"Omigosh!" the woman screamed.

"The good news," the boy continued, "is that the frog he swallowed is real small."

■ ■ ■

The aspiring performer made a rash promise to the circus owner: he said he could train a lion to do a magnificent trick. He was hired, and there was good news: he had trained a lion to eat off his hand. On opening night, the bad news was that the lion did.

■ ■ ■

The magician was depressed when he got home.

"What's wrong?" his wife asked.

"To be honest," he said, "there's bad news and good news.

"The bad news is, I accidentally cut my assistant in half."

"For real?" his wife gasped.

The magician nodded. "The good news, though, is that she's gone to recuperate with her daughters in New York and Chicago."

■ ■ ■

While wandering around a field a little boy found a bullet and swallowed it. His mother rushed him to the doctor, where she was told that there was good news and bad news.

"The good news is, the laxative I gave your boy will relieve him of the bullet sometime tomorrow.

■ ■ ■

"The bad news is, you don't want to be standing behind him anytime today."

"The good news," the lawyer told his friend, "is that I just engineered a deal for my client to work on a project with Ford.

"The bad news," he continued, "is that the project is making license plates in San Quentin."

■ ■ ■

The scientist sat in front of the congressional committee researching the depletion of the ozone layer of the atmosphere.

"The good news," said the scientist, "is that I find it very rewarding to speak to a learned and interested group about the problems facing our environment.

"The bad news," he said, "is that I've got to talk to *you* dunderheads instead. . . ."

■ ■ ■

The theater critic said, "There's good news and bad news about the show that opened last night at the Albert.

"The good news is, the play really moved the audience.

"The bad news is, they moved into the lobby."

■ ■ ■

The biblical scholar studied the Good Book for years, and finally announced this momentous discovery to his fellow scholars:

"I have good news and bad news about the Old Testament. The good news is, it wasn't the apple that got Adam and Eve thrown out of Eden. The bad news is, it was the 'pair' beneath it."

■ ■ ■

The doctor said to his patient, "I have good news and bad news for you. Which do you want first?"

"The bad," said the patient.

"Okay. The bad news is, we're going to have to operate on you."

"Good Lord," said the patient. "What's the *good* news?"

The doctor said, "I bowled a '300' game last night."

■ ■ ■

The phone rang and Mr. Jenkins picked it up; it was his doctor.

"I have good news and bad news," the doctor said. "Which do you want first?"

"The good," said the patient.

"Okay. The good news is, you've only got twenty-four hours to live."

The patient went pale. "That's the *good* news? So what's the bad news, then?"

The doctor replied, "I've been trying to reach you since yesterday."

■ ■ ■

Another doctor went to see his patient Bruno, who had been in a terrible motorcycle accident.

"I have good news and bad news," the doctor said. "The bad news is, we're going to have to cut off your legs."

"I see," said Bruno, putting on his tough biker face. "And what's the good news?"

The doctor answers, "The guy in the next bed wants to buy your boots."

Rock was telling some friends about what he'd done the night before.

"The good news was, I went out with my sister's best friend—very impressive '10'!

"The bad news was, her daddy joined us with *his* best friend—very impressive .45!"

■ ■ ■

The good news was that the new home-care product was the most effective lemon rinse ever made. The bad news was, it didn't sell. No one wanted to rinse their lemons. . . .

■ ■ ■

The pharmacist said to her customer, "The good thing about this new medication is that it will cure your headache in seconds.

"The bad thing," she continued, "is that it takes an hour to get all the cotton out of the bottle."

■ ■ ■

The pharmacist said to another customer, "The good thing about this laxative is that it's very effective.

"The bad thing is that it makes you so weak you can't get out of bed."

The actor said to his friend, "The good news is that my agent has offices in a dozen places abroad.

"The bad news is, now I can be unemployed in twelve countries."

■ ■ ■

"I've got bad news and good news," the pilot said as he stepped from the cockpit, a parachute on his back.

"The bad news is, we've lost power in three of our four engines.

"The good news is, I'm going for help."

■ ■ ■

The copilot's voice came over the intercom. "I have bad news and good news.

"The bad news is, we're going to be forced to make an emergency landing in Iraq.

"The good news is, we'll be arriving ahead of schedule."

■ ■ ■

The lawyer called his client, who was getting divorced.

"I have good news and bad news," the attorney said. "The good news is, I got you half of the house."

"That's terrific! What's the bad news?"

The lawyer said, "You got the outside."

■ ■ ■

Wishing to learn more about his ancestors, Irving went to his grandparents' hometown in Poland and discovered that there was good news and bad news.

The good news was he was able to find out all about his family tree.

The bad news was that many of his relatives were still living in it.

■ ■ ■

The Victorian nobleman went to the home of Mrs. Burton and said, "Madam—I have good news and bad news.

"The good news is that in view of your husband's explorations of the Dark Continent, the Queen has made him a knight."

"How lovely!" Mrs. Burton said. "What's the bad news?"

"The bad news is, the last bunch of natives he discovered made him an angel."

■ ■ ■

Little Kevin came home to the ranch and said, "Ma—I've got bad news and good news.

"The good news is, I got me some pets—a girl snake and a boy snake."

"No way!" his mother shot back. "I don't mind a couple of snakes, but these two will make baby snakes."

"Not to worry, Mom," said the boy. "The good news is, these won't multiply: they're adders."

■ ■ ■

Little Kevin got rid of the snakes and came home with another pet.

"Got bad news and good news about this one, too," he told his mother.

"The bad news is that it's a skunk."

"Forget it!" his mother yelled, "It'll stink up the house."

"No, it won't. I clunked it on the head a few times and now it makes no scents."

■ ■ ■

The tourists in India were traveling in the wilds when, suddenly, a circle of snakes formed behind them.

"Don't worry, there's good news!" said one of the tourists, whipping out a flute. "I'm a snake charmer."

He started playing a haunting tune when, just as suddenly, one of the snakes leaped at him.

"The bad news," said the snake before biting him, "is that I'm deaf."

■ ■ ■

The realtor was showing the couple the house.

"The bad news," he said, "is that the house is in pretty rotten shape.

"But the good news," he continued, "is that the termites eat out."

■ ■ ■

"The good news," the teacher said to the boy's parents, "is that he keeps his shoulder to the wheel, his ear to the ground, and his nose to the grindstone.

"The bad news is, he's got *terrible* posture."

■ ■ ■

Following a space flight, the astronaut had itchy feet and went to see the NASA doctor.

"I've got good news for you," said the medic. "You don't have athlete's foot."

"Great. What *do* I have?"

The doctor said, "That's the bad news: you've got missile toe!"

APARTMENT
GOOD NEWS/BAD NEWS ...

The landlord said to one of his tenants, "I have good news and bad news.

"The good news is, you don't have to move to have a fancier apartment.

"The bad news is, I'm raising the rent on this one."

■ ■ ■

The tenant said to a prospective new neighbor, "The good news about this apartment building is that they allow children.

"The bad news is, the rooms are too small for anyone larger."

■ ■ ■

One landlord was complaining to another landlord. "You know that filthy artist who moved into my building? There's good news and bad news about the lady. The good news is, she's quite an artist.

"The bad news is, all she draws are flies.

... AND SOME ARMY
GOOD NEWS/BAD NEWS

The chef was drafted. His first day at boot camp, the drill sergeant told him, "Bub—I've got good news and bad news for you.

"The good news is, I'm givin' you a free hand when it comes to creatin' meals for the men.

"The bad news is, the kitchen's a mess."

■ ■ ■

Next, the drill sergeant approached Private Lyves.

"I've got bad news and good news for you, too," said the sergeant. "The bad news is, you're going to be stationed where the bullets are thickest."

"Oh, no—"

"The good news is, you're workin' the ammunition depot."

■ ■ ■

The soldiers were camping in the wild when the sergeant said to them, "Listen up! I have some good news and some bad news for you.

"The good news is, tomorrow you get to change your underwear.

"The bad news is—Greg, you're changing with Sam. Mike, you're changing with Ryan. Griff, you're changing with Bob. . . ."

■ ■ ■

The sergeant addressed his outfit before a march through stormy weather.

"Men," he said, "there's good news and bad news about the hiking boots you were issued.

"The good news is they're completely waterproof.

"The bad news is, that means none of the rain is comin' back *out* again."

■ ■ ■

The soldier had been tried and found guilty of treason, and was to be executed. Trying to break it to him easily, his legal counsel said, "Private Hargrove—I have bad news and good news for you.

"The bad news is, we all have to go out on a little march tomorrow at dawn.

"The good news is, you only have to go one way."

■ ■ ■

The soldier still didn't get it, so the lawyer said, "The bad news is, we all have to go into battle tomorrow. The good news is, you won't have to fight."

"The good news about Mr. Detter," said his friend, "is that whenever I lend him money, he says, 'I'm forever in your debt.'

"The bad news is, he means exactly that."

■ ■ ■

The police didn't know how to break it to Mrs. Stimson that her husband had fallen off a balcony and died during a convention in Las Vegas.

Unable to stall any longer, the officer phoned the widow.

"Ma'am," he said, "I've got good news and bad news. The good news is that your husband came to town and didn't lose a penny. . . ."

■ ■ ■

The day after his Broadway debut, the actor picked up the paper and read good news and bad news.

The good news was that he was being compared with the great actors of the past.

The bad news was, unfavorably.

■ ■ ■

GOOD NEWS/BAD NEWS
FOR WRITERS . . .

After suing the publisher for allegedly infringing on his copyrighted story, the author returned home.

"How did it go?" his wife asked.

"I have good news and bad news," replied the writer. "The good news is, I got five dollars a word."

"That's wonderful!" she said, hugging him.

"The bad news," he continued, "is that it's a fine for yelling at the judge."

■ ■ ■

The author's agent called the controversial writer and said, "I have good news and bad news.

"The good news is, your new novel is moving like wildfire.

"The bad news is, that's because people are burning it."

■ ■ ■

"The good news," said the author, "is that my agent and I get along much better if we go on vacation at least twice a year.

"The bad news is, she goes to one place and I go to another."

■ ■ ■

Then there was the convict who decided to do something with his time. The good news was he decided to write a book about his experiences in prison. The bad news was, it took him a year to finish one sentence. (Maybe he should have written escapist fiction!)

■ ■ ■

And we mustn't forget the author who finally made some money from writing. That was the good news.

The bad news was, he was writing bad checks. . . .

. . . AND ARTISTS

The artist came running through the door.

"Honey, I've got news—good news and bad news!"

"What is it?"

"The good news," he said, "is that I got money for the painting I sent to Lord Raindon."

"How wonderful!"

"The bad news," he said, "is that it's from the post office for losing it."

■ ■ ■

After years of struggle, the despondent illustrator said to his girlfriend, "I have good news and bad news.

"The good news is, the Society of Artists finally accepted something of mine.

"The bad news is, it was my resignation."

The two gossips were talking.

"Have you heard about Jezebel?"

"No, what about her?"

"The good news is, I hear she went on a crash diet."

"Good for her!"

"The bad news is, she looks like a wreck."

■ ■ ■

The car salesperson said, "If you're interested in a super-mini-compact, there's good news and bad news.

"The good news is, these babies stop on a dime.

"The bad news is, that's because they can't get over them."

Little Ricky said to his friend, "I got some good news and bad news and worse news this week.

"The good news is that I got a baby brother.

"The bad news is that it's so ugly, the stork had to bring it at night.

"It's so ugly, in fact, that the worse news is my parents powdered the wrong end all week without realizing it."

■ ■ ■

The accountant reported to the corporate chairperson, "Sir, I've got good news and bad news.

"The good news is, I've discovered that there's only one way to keep our bills down.

"The bad news is, it's a paperweight."

■ ■ ■

The nurse came running to see the doctor in the maternity ward.

"Dr. Charles," she said, "I have good news and bad news about the Addams baby.

"The good news is, his dad just came to visit and gave him a rattle."

"Hmmm," said the doctor. "There's nothing wrong with that."

"The bad news," she continued, "is that it was still attached to the snake."

■ ■ ■

"The good news," the man told his friend, "was that my wife found a hundred-dollar bill stuffed in the desk.

"The bad news is, now I've got to pay it."

■ ■ ■

The accountant called his client.

"Good news, Mick," he said. "Even if the recession keeps up, it isn't going to affect you."

"That's great," said Mick, "but how come?"

The accountant said, "That's the bad news: you're broke."

■ ■ ■

The two elderly men were reminiscing.

"When I hit sixty, there was good news," said one. "My hair had gone white as snow."

"That was *good* news?" his friend asked.

The man nodded. "The bad news was that by the time I hit seventy, someone had shoveled it all off."

■ ■ ■

The scientist said to his assistant, "Good news! I've figured out how to make an elephant fly! The bad news is, I don't know where to find two yards of zipper."

■ ■ ■

The banker opened a branch office near a cemetery, and told potential depositors that there was bad news and good news.

The bad news is, you can't take it with you.

The good news is, you can be *very* close to it.

■ ■ ■

Ralph, a lazy young opportunist, overheard a woman talking in a bar about how her daddy's health was failing and she didn't know what she was going to do with the bank he owned.

Ralph ingratiated himself with the woman, married her, then got the good news and bad news: the good news was that he'd misunderstood, her daddy's health was fine. The bad news was that the bank was failing.

■ ■ ■

The good news was that the ugly girl finally got married. The bad news was, she was *so* ugly, all she could get was the honeymoon sour.

■ ■ ■

Balding Mr. Exhirsute walked into the barbershop.

"You should have some good news for me," said the man. "Like—it'll cost me less because I have less hair."

"On the contrary," said the barber, "I have some bad news for you. This will cost you more because I have to go *searching* for it."

■ ■ ■

The very nearsighted Mr. Bean was relaxing on the beach in Hawaii when he got up and approached a man roasting a pig on a spit.

"Good news," said Mr. Bean. "Your organ hasn't bothered me a bit. Bad news, though, is I think your monkey is burning."

■ ■ ■

The police officer said to the chief, "I've got bad news and good news about Schmidt.

"The bad news is, we can't find him, the woman he kidnapped, the car he stole, or any trace of the fifty grand he robbed.

"The good news is, they've found someone to teach his Sunday-school class."

■ ■ ■

Benjamin, a builder, hired a new employee. After his first day on the job, Benjamin went over to him and said, "I have good news and bad news.

"The good news is, you hammer those nails like lightning."

"Am I *really* that good?"

"Not really," said Benjamin. "The bad news is, you never strike the same place twice."

■ ■ ■

The good news: the elderly gentleman saved up a little something for a rainy day.

The bad news: it was a rubber check.

■ ■ ■

The outlaw came galloping into camp and dropped four saddlebags full of money next to the campfire.

"Boss, there's good news and bad news," said the bandit. "The good news is, the bank robbery went exactly as planned."

"So what's the bad news?" the boss asked.

The outlaw replied, "That's the bank where we keep all of *our* money."

■ ■ ■

The little old man found a magic lantern in the desert and rubbed it. A genie emerged and offered the old man one wish.

"A wish?" the old man said, then shouted, "I don't want to be an old man anymore!"

A GOOD NEWS/BAD NEWS FIGHT STORY

There was good news for Kid McGraw, the boxer: he convinced a promoter he could beat the heavyweight champ, hands down.

The bad news was, the champ never *kept* them down.

■ ■ ■

The good news for Kid McGraw, though, was that he brought the champ to his knees in the very first round.

The bad news was, the champ was checking to see if the challenger was still breathing.

■ ■ ■

The sportswriters, at least, felt there was good news: they said the challenger was a colorful fighter. The bad news, though, was that the colors were black and blue.

■ ■ ■

McGraw didn't let this little setback get him down, and the good news was that he managed to make a great deal of money in other fights. The bad news was, he did it by selling ad space on the soles of his shoes.

The good news is that he got what he asked for. The bad news is, now he's an old woman.

■ ■ ■

Durwood said to his wife, "Remember how you complained to the landlord that there's never enough water to fill the bathtub completely?"

"Of course I do."

"Well, I've got good news and bad news. The good news is, the problem's been taken care of. The bad news is, he moved the bathtub under the hole in the roof."

■ ■ ■

Then there was the teenager whose mother went to a new beauty parlor and—good news!—came out looking twenty years younger. So the teen went and—bad news!—she disappeared.

■ ■ ■

The Great Aqua showed up at the circus manager's tent and said he had a great attraction for his sideshow.

"The good news," said Aqua, "is that I can empty a six-pack of Coke with a single swallow."

"That's impressive," said the manager.

Aqua went on, "The bad news is, after that the poor bird burps for a month!"

SOME BASEBALL
GOOD NEWS/BAD NEWS ...

Tony and Peter went to the baseball game, and almost at once, the opposing team scored two runs. In the second inning, they scored another two.

Disgusted, Peter left to make a phone call. When he returned, he asked, "Anything happen?"

"Truth is," said Tony, "there's good news and bad news. The good news is, one of our guys slid into home."

"We got some hits?" Peter asked, squinting up at the scoreboard.

"Not exactly," said Tony. "The bad news is, he was coming up to bat."

■ ▪ ■

Then there was the pitcher who experienced a good news/bad news night: the good news was that he finally won a game and celebrated until the wee hours of the morning. The bad news was, he got thrown out at home.

■ ▪ ■

And we mustn't forget the baseball player who gave the sportswriters some very good news to write about: he masterminded a no-hitter.

The bad news was, he was in a brawl at the time.

■ ■ ■

Newlywed Martha came into work looking glum as can be.

"What's wrong?" a coworker asked. "A whirlwind romance, a good-looking husband—what have you got to be sad about?"

"Remember when I told you that when we were wed my husband-to-be was going to treat me to one of the biggest diamonds in America?"

"I do—"

"That was the good news. The bad news is, he took me to see a Yankees game."

... AND FOOTBALL
GOOD NEWS/BAD NEWS

After scouting the college teams, Benson reported back to the general manager.

"Find anyone good out there?" Benson was asked.

The scout said, "There's good news and bad news about our finest prospect, a quarterback named Jones. The good news is he can throw the ball one hundred yards."

The general manager's jaw dropped. "You signed him, right?"

Benson said, "No, sir. The bad news is, he can only throw the ball straight *up*."

The two cons were talking in prison.

"I've wasted so much of my life," said one. "The good news is that when I get out of here, I plan to open a coin shop.

"The bad news is, I don't know *where* I'm going to get the proper tools."

■ ■ ■

The college student was panhandling in town.

"Mister," he said to a passerby, "want to hear some bad news? I haven't eaten in so long I forgot what food *tastes* like."

The passerby replied, "Want to hear some good news? It still tastes the same."

■ ■ ■

"Pop," said little Oliver, "do you like your job?"

A SHORT BUSINESS STORY

Then there was the unemployed Ph.D. who went looking for a job. A headhunter said, "Good news! I've got a job for you that fills the bill."

The Ph.D. took it, only to discover the bad news—that the job was feeding ducks at a petting zoo.

The man answered, "There's bad news and good news about being a cabdriver.

"The bad news is, you have to drive through crowded streets.

"The good news is, I like a lot of the people I run into."

■ ■ ■

Al went to dinner at the local grease pit and noticed a sign: WATCH YOUR COAT. The good news was, he kept an eye on it and no one touched it.

The bad news was, someone snatched his dinner.

■ ■ ■

"There's good news and bad news about our baby daughter," Mrs. Ogan told her friend.

"The good news is, we have a pet name for her.

"The bad news is, that's because she looks like one."

■ ■ ■

"The bad news," another cabdriver said to the police, "is that—yes, I had a fight with my mother-in-law, drove her to another state, and just *left* her there.

"But the good news is, I didn't leave the meter running."

■ ■ ■

"The good news," said the restaurant goer, "is that the chic new Raw Food Restaurant on Columbus Avenue accepts cards.

"The bad news is, they're Blue Cross and Blue Shield."

■ ■ ■

The car salesperson told a customer, "The good news is, I stand behind every single car I sell."

Overhearing him, the service manager whispered, "The bad news is, that's because the brakes don't always work."

■　■　■

Doing the radiocast for the football game, Frank Meredith said, "Ohhh! There's good news and bad news, folks.

"The good news is, Lance Brown just broke a half-dozen tackles to carry the ball an incredible thirty-seven yards.

"The bad news is, it was his own guys trying to stop him from running the wrong way."

■　■　■

Then there was longtime bachelor Quentin, who told a friend that there was good news and bad news about being married. The good news was, whenever his wife displeased him, Quentin had every right to complain.

The bad news was, after the first time, he no longer had the nerve.

■　■　■

Mr. Brady said to a coworker, "You want to hear some good news? That unbreakable wagon I got for my kid's birthday really *is* unbreakable!

"The bad news is, I broke my car when I ran over it."

The guard ran in to the warden's office.

"Sir, there's good news and bad news. The good news is, there's poison ivy growing in the compound."

"That's *good* news? It sounds like bad news to me."

"No, sir. The bad news is, several of the convicts have broken out."

■ ■ ■

After deciding that he wanted to break up with his business partner, Warren said to his wife, "I've got good news and bad news.

"The good news is, it was a clean fifty-fifty split.

"The bad news is, my partner got half and my lawyer got the other half."

■ ■ ■

Jonathan's girlfriend, Jackie, came over for dinner. When they sat down at the table, she was amazed at how well behaved the dog was.

"The good news," said Jonathan, "is that he *never* comes to the table and begs."

Jackie took a bite and said, "The bad news is, that's because he's tasted your cooking."

■ ■ ■

Hoping to enter show business, the mind reader left North Dakota for Hollywood.

"The good news," she wrote home, "is that the weather is beautiful.

"The bad news is, I'm unable to practice my trade here."

■ ■ ■

"The good news," the woman said to her friend, "was that for their fiftieth wedding anniversary, my father told my mother she'd see the world, just like she'd always wanted.

"The bad news is, he bought her a globe."

■ ■ ■

"The good news," Reginald said to a friend, "was that I got my younger brother something really fun for his birthday—a bat.

"The bad news was, it flew off."

■ ■ ■

Phil said to his friend Carl, "You look lost in thought. What's up?"

Carl said, "I met a woman and I can't decide whether or not to marry her. The good news is, she's an old-fashioned girl who cooks just like my grandmother.

"The bad news is, she looks just like my grandfather."

When Mr. Savran came home from work, Mrs. Savran said, "Honey—there's bad news and good news.

"The bad news is, for his science project, little Michael has to raise a skunk to adulthood."

"What about the *stink*?" said Mr. Savran.

Mrs. Savran said, "That's the good news: the skunk seems to be getting used to it."

■ ■ ■

"The bad news," said little Suzie, "is that my great-great-grandma is so old it takes *forever* to put the candles on her birthday cake.

"The good news is, when they're lit, the cake cooks itself."

■ ■ ■

One landlord said to another, "You want to know the good news about Mrs. Jenkins? She always pays her rent with a smile.

"The bad news is, I'd prefer cash."

■ ■ ■

After trying on a slick new suit, Lawrence said to the salesclerk, "The good news is, clothes *do* make the man.

"The bad news is, the price breaks him."

■ ▓ ■

Muriel was saying to her friend, "The good news was, my husband said he was going to surprise me for Christmas.

"The bad news is, he woke up on December 25th and said, 'Boo!' "

■ ▓ ■

"How was your cross-country drive?" Willard asked his coworker Barb.

"There was bad news and good news," she said. "The bad news was, there was a *terrible* noise in the car for the first half of the trip.

"The good news was, it stopped when we left my mother at the Grand Canyon."

■ ▓ ■

"The good news," the lawyer told his client, "is that your case is now in the hands of twelve ordinary, hardworking folks like yourself."

"The bad news," said the client, "is that not one of the dozen was smart enough to get *out* of jury duty."

■ ▓ ■

The flood caused a strain on emergency services in the town, and people were being helped according to need.

"You've got to get here quick," said one caller."

"Are you in immediate danger?"

"Well, the good news is I'm only standing in a foot of it—"

"Then you'll have to wait awhile, I'm afraid."

The caller continued, "The bad news is, I'm on the third floor."

■ ■ ■

On his birthday, the doctor came to see the man with amnesia.

"The good news," said the doctor, "is that I've brought you a present.

"The bad news," she said, "is that I still can't give you a past."

■ ■ ■

The head of the charity organization said to a new volunteer, "The good news about billionaire Hughes is that on every holiday, he remembers the poor.

"The bad news is, that's *all* he does."

■ ■ ■

"The good news," said the salesclerk, "is that this computer is *very* high tech.

"The bad news is, I mean the price is high."

■ ■ ■

The two waiters were conferring about their regular customer Mr. Penny.

"The good news about him is that he always leaves a tip.

"The bad news is, it's things like, 'Don't leave home without an umbrella' and 'Call your mother once a week.' "

■ ■ ■

"The good news," said Mrs. Quirk, "is that for the first time in his cheap life, the meal was on my dad.

"The bad news is, that's because the waiter dropped it in his lap."

■ ■ ■

The guidance counselor said to Mr. and Mrs. Tobin, "I have good news and bad news about Sarah.

"The good news is, the kids love your freckled little girl!

"The bad news is, they like to play connect-the-dots on her face."

■ ■ ■

"The good news," said the salesclerk in the clothing store, "is that you can wear these boots in the rain.

"The bad news is, your feet will get soaked—but you can still wear them."

■ ■ ■

The college student wrote back to his parents, "The good news is, I'm going to be wading through over fifty books this year.

"The bad news is, half of them will be checkbooks."

■ ■ ■

Then there was the college kid who wrote home to his parents, "I've got good news and bad news.

"The good news is, next semester, my education will cost you zippo.

"The bad news is, I flunked out."

■ ■ ■

Mr. Lee invited the new neighbors over for dinner, telling them, "The good news is that I *really* appreciate my wife's cooking.

"The bad news is, just yesterday I was able to patch the wall with her oatmeal and polish the silver with her sponge cake."

■ ■ ■

Isaac said to an acquaintance, "The good news is, my friend Ben plays a mean game of racquetball.

"The bad news is, he aims the ball at the back of your head."

■ ■ ■

Old Mrs. Dinsdale said to her nephew, "The good news, Roderick, is that I drive so slowly I have *never* been given a speeding ticket."

Her husband, Mr. Dinsdale, remarked, "The bad news is, she *has* been ticketed by troopers who thought she was parked on the highway."

■ ■ ■

"The good news," said the woman, glancing into the mirror, "is that my figure is still a legend."

"The bad news," said her snide husband, "is that the legend is starting to spread."

■ ■ ■

The scientist told his colleague, "I have good news, Fritz. I've discovered that a diet of potassium and phosphorus kills cold germs.

"The bad news is, I haven't figured out how to get those buggers to *eat* it."

■ ■ ■

Kate met an old friend for lunch.

"Remember Ken?" said Kate. "The bad news is, I'm no longer engaged to him."

"You mean that crude, snide, chauvinistic, dog-hating, Norman Mailer—reading jerk?"

"That's the one. The good news is, we're married."

■ ■ ■

"The good news," Todd told his friend Ryan, "is that I got a dog to keep from getting robbed.

"The bad news is, I got mugged while I was out walking him."

■ ■ ■

The banker said, "The good news is, at our bank we no longer put up those obnoxious signs that say, 'Next teller please.'

"The bad news is, the signs now say, 'Next bank please.' "

■ ■ ■

"I've got good news and bad news," the attorney said to his client. "The good news is, I got you a suspended sentence.

"The bad news is, you hang in the morning."

■ ■ ■

Then there was Max, who killed his boss in a fit of rage. His attorney came to visit him after the trial, and said, "Good news! The judge gave you just one month in prison."

"For killing my boss?" said Max. "That's amazing. What's the bad news?"

"The bad news," said the lawyer, "is that when the month is over, you get the hot seat."

■ ■ ■

Tony saw his friend Riff at the mall.

"Hey, how come we never see you here anymore?"

"Well," said Riff, "the bad news is, my mom's making me take ballet lessons so I'll learn some discipline."

"Yuck-o," said Tony.

"Yeah," said Riff. "The good news is, I'm getting better by leaps and bounds."

■ ■ ■

The waiter at the club frequented by heavy-metal artists and producers was telling his friend, "The bad news is, last night I dropped a tray loaded with plates, glasses, and flatware.

"The good news is, I got a two-year recording contract."

■ ■ ■

In the locker room at the tennis court, Woodrow asked Kingsley, "How's your game been?"

Kingsley replied, "There's good news and bad news. The good news is, for the first half hour, I ace every serve I make."

"That's an improvement over last year," Woodrow pointed out.

"The bad news is, then my opponent shows up."

■ ■ ■

"The good news," Dr. Klein said to Dr. Trias, "is that old Mr. Winkle is really fighting his arthritis. I give him a lot of credit.

"The bad news is, I have to. He's got no insurance."

■ ■ ■

"The good news," Oliver said to his accountant, "is that I've just started on my second million dollars.

"The bad news is, I've given up on trying to make the first million."

■ ■ ■

The businesswoman said to her friend over lunch, "The good news is, the recession hasn't affected me a bit.

"The bad news is, I went broke when the economy was in good shape."

■ ■ ■

Clarence told his wife, "There's bad news, good news, and bad news," he said.

"The bad news is, our business is on the verge of failing.

"The good news is, the accountant stopped by and told me to think positive.

"The bad news is, I did: now I'm positive it's on the verge of failing."

■ ■ ■

The two dimwits were riding the roller coaster.

"The good news," said one, "is that we're making great time."

"Yes," said the other. "The bad news is, I don't think this is the right bus."

■ ■ ■

The doctor said to Melvin, "There's bad news, good news, and bad news.

"The bad news is, your left leg is shorter than your right.

"The good news is, there's something you can do for it.

"The bad news is, it's limp."

■ ■ ■

"The good news," the chef told a friend, "is that my new dog absolutely *loves* garlic.

"The bad news is that now her bark really is worse than her bite!"

■ ■ ■

Mrs. Berkowitz said to her friend, "The good news is, the doctor said that walking the dog is good for weight loss.

"The bad news is, who wants a skinny dog?"

■ ■ ■

One caveman said to the other, "Good news, Tumak. Me going out to hunt for duckosaurus.

"Bad news—need you to help me carry five-ton decoy."

■ ■ ■

Bill said to his neighbor Frank, "Congratulations! I hear you've been elected dogcatcher."

"I have," said Frank, "and that's the good news. The bad news is, I have no idea what I'm supposed to catch them *doing*."

■ ■ ■

The mayor decided to endorse the senator for reelection.

"The good news," said the mayor, "is that our senator has done the work of three men."

"The bad news," shouted an onlooker, "is that they're Moe, Larry, and Curly."

■ ■ ■

"I'm a lucky guy," Waldo said to his friend. "The good news is, there's never a dull moment in my life.

"The bad news is, there are a lot of dull *years* in my life. . . ."

■ ■ ■

Lou said to Bud, "I got a new dog, and boy, is he something!"

"How do you mean?"

"Well, the good news is, he can read.

"The bad news is, he saw a sign that said, 'Wet Paint,' and he did!"

■ ■ ■

Miranda had to be at a meeting in less than an hour, so she took the company car instead of the train. When she arrived, she phoned her boss and said, "There's good news and bad news, Mr. Delacort. The good news is, I made it.

"The bad news is, I drove like lightning."

"Hmmm . . . are you telling me you got a speeding ticket?"

"No," she said. "I struck a tree."

■ ■ ■

After Myron left the party, the host said to his wife, "The good news is, Myron lights up a room—"

His wife said, "The bad news is, by *leaving* it."

■ ■ ■

The elderly Renee was telling a friend, "The good news is, men still throw themselves at my feet."

"The bad news," said her friend, "is that's because they can't stand your face."

■ ■ ■

The ice on the pond broke, and young Kent stood there calling for help.

"What's wrong?" shouted a passerby. "The water only comes up to your waist!"

"You're right," said Kent. "The good news is I'm in no immediate danger of drowning. The bad news is, the guy whose shoulders I'm standing on *is*."

■ ■ ■

After visiting the doctor, Murray came home and told his wife, "Good news! The doctor said I have the body of an eighteen-year-old."

"Really?" his wife said.

"Sort of," Murray continued. "The bad news is he meant dog."

■ ■ ■

Telling a new employee about their boss, the secretary said, "The good news is, there's a lot of good in Ms. Bredice.

"The bad news is, she never lets it out."

■ ■ ■

After surviving the tornado, the young couple told the reporter, "The good news is that as soon as we heard it was coming, we headed to the next county.

"The bad news is, our house got there before we did."

■ ■ ■

"The good news," a fisherman said to the newcomer, "is that the fish are biting today.

"The bad news is, it's each other they're biting!"

■ ■ ■

Announcing that he intended to run for President, the senator told the reporters, "The good news is, I'm a candidate who intends to stand on his record."

A COLLEGE TALE

"Who says our athletes aren't getting a good college education?" Dean Halsey roared at the English teacher Professor Moran.

"Well," said the professor, "look at the school quarterback, Darien West. The good news is, he got his varsity letter.

"The bad news is, I had to read it to him."

■ ■ ■

Upon hearing this, the dean was furious. "You can't be right about West. Why, the good news is that just today he told me he *never* gets tired of thinking!"

"The bad news," said Moran, "is that's because he never does any."

■ ■ ■

Dean Halsey roared, "You're wrong! The good news is that West has an open mind."

Moran replied, "The bad news is, it's not just open . . . it's empty."

A journalist quipped, "The bad news is, that's so we can't look into it."

■　■　■

Thompson applied for a new job, but was turned down after his prospective employer read the recommendation his previous boss had sent over.

"It says here there's good news and bad news about you, Thompson. The good news is that you made fewer mistakes than any accountant in your company's history."

"So why won't you hire me?"

" 'Cause of the bad news," she replied. "It says you made fewer mistakes because you showed up at noon and left at three."

■　■　■

"The good news," Peter said to his pal Jolie, "is that my wife makes the sourest, muddiest coffee on earth."

"Why is that good news?" Jolie asked.

Peter said, "Because then I never notice how runny the eggs are."

■　■　■

"The goods news," old Nehemiah told his friend old Jake, "is that I've saved my money for a rainy day.

"The bad news is, my arthritis is so bad when it rains, I can't go anywhere to spend it."

■ ■ ■

Morty told his neighbor, "You want to hear some good news? I woke up this morning with a real itch to rake every leaf in the yard.

"The bad news is, I stayed in bed till the itch went away."

■ ■ ■

Carlton was telling a friend about the girl he'd dated the night before.

"The good news," he said, "is that her skin was as smooth as a petal."

"Rose?" asked the friend.

Carlton shook his head. "That's the bad news—I mean bicycle."

■ ■ ■

Sally said, "The good news is, I get myself a new dress whenever I'm down in the dumps.

"The bad news is, they smell of garbage for *days* after that."

■ ■ ■

Mr. and Mrs. Bova were chatting over dinner.

"I have good news, honey," said Mrs. Bova. "Ever since we started giving little Seth an allowance, he's really learned the value of a dollar.

"The bad news," she went on, "is that now he wants us to pay him in German marks."

■ ■ ■

"The good news," the woman said to the school principal, "is that my little Jimmy would *never* stoop to anything so low as you just described."

"Ah," said the principal, "but the bad news is that he's so low-down he doesn't *have* to stoop."

■ ■ ■

When Mr. Benn arrived at the office, he told his secretary, "The good news is that I had some delicious coffee this morning with milk and one lump.

"The bad news is, the lump was my teen-age son."

■ ■ ■

After the fifth round of the championship fight, the trainer said to the battered boxer, "There's good news and bad news.

"The good news is, you've finally stopped bleeding.

"The bad news is, you're all out of blood."

■ ■ ■

Newlywed Max said to his friend, "The good news is that my bride is constantly searching through magazines for new recipes.

"The bad news is, the magazines are *Mad, Rip,* and *Dog Fancy.*"

■ ■ ■

"The good news," Adam said to Eve, "is that tomorrow is the first holiday in the history of the world!

"The bad news is, I have *no* idea what to buy for Father's Day."

■ ■ ■

The teacher sat down with Mr. and Mrs. Rachlin.

"The good news," she said, "is that little Neil doesn't know the first thing about fighting, spitting, cursing, cutting class, or the other things bad children do."

The Rachlins smiled.

"The bad news," the teacher went on, "is that he does them anyway."

■ ■ ■

"The good news," one of the twins said to their ugly new baby-sitter, "is that you're going to be great at playing peek-a-boo."

"Really?" She smiled.

"The bad news," said the other twin, "is that one peek at your puss and we're gonna boo!"

■ ■ ■

"The good news," the police officer said to the shopkeeper after the robbery, "is that your loved ones are all safe and secure.

"The bad news is that the rest of your money is gone."

■ ■ ■

After listening for hours to the musical racket coming from the apartment above, Paul went upstairs to tell the musician to cool it—gently, though, since he knew how temperamental artists could be.

"I have good news and bad news," Paul said. "The good news is that you play the flute splendidly."

"But these are drums, man," the musician said.

Paul said, "That's the bad news."

■ ■ ■

On the occasion of his one-hundredth birthday, Old Vincent told his ninety-year-old friend Rob, "There's good news and bad news about being this old. The good news is that my wife and I just celebrated our cardboard anniversary."

"You doddering old fool! There's no such thing as a cardboard anniversary."

"Oh, yes, there is," said Vincent, "and that's the bad news. All we did was play cards and be bored."

■ ■ ■

Freddy showed up for his checkup, and the doctor was disturbed that he hadn't lost any weight in six months. After discussing the problem with Freddy, the doctor said, "I've got some good news and bad news for you.

"The good news is, what I told you last visit still holds true: a few hours of basketball a week will cause you to lose weight.

"The bad news is, I meant playing . . . not watching."

■ ■ ■

The President of the United States told the Congress, "The good news is that I've decided to use the military to enforce my will in the Middle East.

"The bad news is, I mean Washington, D.C."

■ ■ ■

"The good news," Dave told his wife, "is that your brother is a man of his word: he said he'd never forget that I was the one who bailed him out of jail last week.

"The bad news is, he's just called me to do it again."

■ ■ ■

"Oh, there's such good news!" Mrs. Periwinkle said to her friend. "I entered my little kitty in the cat beauty contest and—look! I won the first prize ribbon."

"That's very nice."

"Yes, but there's bad news too: I suppose it would have been better if kitty was the one to win."

■ ■ ■

The insurance companies and the airlines issued a joint communiqué about the drop in fares and the rise in insurance:

"The good news is that the cost of going up is going down.

"The bad news is that the cost of going down is going up."

■ ■ ■

After studying the company's books, the accountant said, "Mr. Talbott: I have good news and bad news.

"The good news is, if you hire me, I can

eliminate all of your past debts and save the company.

"The bad news is, I'm so expensive you'll be broke all over again."

■ ■ ■

"My husband went to Las Vegas on a business trip," Millie told her friend, "and the good news is, he never reached into his wallet. He just stood there and made mental bets.

"The bad news is, he lost his mind."

■ ■ ■

"The good news," said the New York art teacher to a colleague, "is that my kids are drawing less and less in class."

"Why is that *good* news?" the colleague asked.

"Because the bad news is, they were drawing guns."

■ ■ ■

Mr. Kahrs listened to hear his granddaughter Susie become frustrated while practicing the violin.

Trying to be reassuring, Mr. Kahrs said, "Susie—the good news is that almost everything gets easier with practice."

"Would you come over and keep reminding me of that?"

Mr. Kahrs shook his head. "The bad news is, getting out of a chair isn't one of them."

■ ■ ■

Later on in the day, Mr. Kahrs was talking to a friend of his.

"Yup," said Kahrs, "the good news is, my vital juices are flowing as strong as ever."

"Sure," said his friend. "The bad news is, they're prune."

■ ■ ■

While making their way through the jungle, the explorer said to a member of his party, "The good news is, the cannibals in the village up ahead are the friendliest people you'll ever meet.

"The bad news is, be ready to run if they break out the glasses and offer to toast you. . . ."

■ ■ ■

"The good news," beautiful teenager Jamie said to her friend, "is that that nerdy Roger said he'd go to the ends of the earth for me."

"That's sweet," said her friend.

"Sure. But the bad news is, he won't stay there."

■ ■ ■

"How was your wedding anniversary?" Mrs. Wiggins asked Mrs. Diggle.

"Well, there's good news and bad news. The good news is, my cheapskate husband promised to get me pearls for our fiftieth anniversary."

"Did you get them?" Mrs. Wiggins asked.

"Sort of," she said. "The bad news is, he gave me an oyster and a rabbit's foot."

■ ■ ■

"So," Marcy said to her friend Julianne, "how is it being married to a geologist?"

"There's good news and bad news," Julianne said. "The good news is, we get to travel all over the world.

"The bad news is, every time we go out, he takes me for granite."

■ ■ ■

The first selectman told the other selectmen, "The good news is, I've figured out how to raise the money for the campaign to keep our town free of gambling.

"The bad news is, it's by selling raffle tickets."

■ ■ ■

"Pop," said the young man, "I've got good news! I just became engaged to a cover girl."

"Wow! She must be something to look at!"

"She sure is. The bad news is, when other guys see her, they run for cover."

■ ■ ■

"How did the showdown with your boyfriend go last week?" Melanie asked Paula.

"Well, the good news is, I told him I wanted a little respect from him.

"The bad news is, that's exactly what he gave me."

■ ■ ■

"The good news," Mrs. Pyncheon said to the doctor, "is that my son doesn't eat between meals.

"The bad news is, he never stops."

■ ■ ■

"So," Joe asked his friend Franklin, "how was your vacation in New York?"

"Oh, there was good news and bad news. The good news is that most of the people were delightful. Why, while I was waiting for a bus one man *very* politely asked me for the time."

"How charming!"

A SHORT CRIME STORY

The young hoodlum ran into his mother's house.

"Mama, Mama, I've got good news and bad news. The good news is, I was out with the boys and scored my first hit!

"The bad news is, it was a pop fly and Rudy caught it."

■ ■ ■

The gangster ran into his mother's house the next night.

"Mama, Mama, there's good news and bad news. The good news is, I pulled off my first bank job.

"The bad news is, I got mugged on my way to the getaway car."

■ ■ ■

For the last time, the gangster ran into his mother's house.

"Mama, Mama, I've got good news and bad news. The good news is, I blew up my first car!

"The bad news is, I burned my mouth on the exhaust."

"Yes. The bad news is he had a gun, so I had to give him my watch."

■ ■ ■

The boss said to his new employee, "Harold, the good news is you're like a son to me.

"The bad news is, I hate my kid."

■ ■ ■

The two ghosts met in the haunted house.

"I have good news and bad news," said one. "The good news is, the Christmas committee has asked me to bring Santa's ghost to this year's party."

"Sounds like fun. What's the bad news?"

"The bad news is, I just don't have that holiday spirit."

■ ■ ■

Freddie told his wife, "Honey—good news! I joined a health club.

"The bad news is, I'm so outta shape, they make me come in the backdoor."

■ ■ ■

Quentin said to his friend Todd, "How was your wife's birthday?"

"There's good news and bad news about

that," Todd said. "The good news is, I bought her a lovely handbag.

"The bad news is, she was expecting a TV."

■ ■ ■

Todd added, "Don't think I'm the only cheapie around. There was good news and bad news on my birthday, too.

"The good news was, my wife promised to buy me something I could drive."

"The bad news is, she bought me a bucket of golf balls."

■ ■ ■

"How was the horse race?" Mrs. Shoemaker asked her husband when he came home.

"There's bad news and good news," he said. "The bad news is, the horse I bet on in the first race may be the slowest animal on earth.

"The good news is, he was so slow he won the second race."

■ ■ ■

"The good news," the golfer told his friend at the club, "is that I get to hit the ball more than anyone else here."

"The bad news," said his friend, "is that you mean in each game."

■ ■ ■

"The good news is that golf is a very inexpensive sport," the golfer also told his friend.

"The bad news is, that's because you never hit a ball far enough to lose it."

■ ■ ■

Jack met his friend Ralph for a hunting trip.

"I can't believe your wife let you go," said Ralph. "I thought she was an animal activist."

"There's bad news and good news about my wife," said Jack. "The bad news is, we had a long, terrible fight before she gave in. The good news is, she felt so bad she gave me this beautiful deerskin jacket before I left. . . ."

■ ■ ■

"The good news," the young man told his pal, "is that with this $4,000 satellite dish, I get to see all the movies I want."

"The bad news," said his friend, "is that they're the same ones you paid only seven bucks to see in the theaters."

■ ■ ■

The actor called his publicist, anxious to hear the reactions to his latest film.

"The good news," said the publicist, "is that everybody in town is talking about it!"

"Hey, that's *great!*" shouted the actor.

"The bad news is, they aren't saying anything good."

■ ■ ■

The surgeon walked up to his patient's bedside.

"How'm I doing, Doc?"

"I've got bad news and good news for you," the surgeon said. "The bad news is, I cut off the wrong arm. The good news is, your bad arm is improving."

■ ■ ■

"Ah," the wealthy woman told her friend, "the good news is that my new husband married for love.

"The bad news is, it was for love of money."

■ ■ ■

"The good news," the teenager told her friend, "is that I've finally found a perfume guaranteed to overpower any guy I meet.

"The bad news is, I'm really going to miss judo."

■ ■ ■

The young man came home from college.

"Pop," he said, "there's good news and bad news. The good news is, I helped to win the big game for the East."

"But I thought you were playing for the West."

"That's the bad news," the young man said. "I was."

■ ■ ■

The teacher phoned young Larry's mother. "Mrs. Fine," she said, "I have good news and bad news. The bad news is, your son has dropped out of school."

"Oh, no!"

"The good news," she said, "is that he was only on the first floor."

■ ■ ■

"The good news," said the teen to his friend, "is that my mom doesn't stay up waiting for me till three in the morning anymore.

"The bad news is, it's because my curfew is midnight."

■ ■ ■

Receiving a postcard from his partner in Spain, Heshy read it to their secretary.

" 'The good news is, I took this trip to forget everything—and I have.

" 'The bad news is, that includes my luggage.' "

■ ■ ■

"The good news," the politician told the gathering, "is that we have free speech in this country."

"The bad news," said someone in the audience, "is that nobody hears you unless you pay to use a phone."

■ ■ ■

Morris was telling a friend about his vacation on an exotic South Pacific island.

"The good news," Morris said, "is that they do everything under the sun there.

"The bad news is, you get *awfully* hot while you're doing it."

■ ■ ■

Lance's mother came to visit her soldier son in the brig.

"What are you *doing* here?" she cried.

"Well, Ma, there's good news and bad news. The good news is, I saved fifty lives."

"You did? So why are you here?"

"The bad news is, I did it by socking the lieutenant who wanted to send us into battle."

Little Peter said to his mom, "I just got my report card, and there's good news and bad news.

"The good news is that I'm just like George Washington and Thomas Jefferson."

"That sounds great!" she said. "In what way?"

"That's the bad news. I went down in history."

■ ■ ■

Little Peter came home after the next marking period and said, "Ma, there's good news and bad news about this one. *This* time the teacher told me I've got a head like Lincoln.

"The bad news is, she meant the monument."

■ ■ ■

Wilson walked up to the local mechanic.

"Guess what, Mac. I've got good news and bad news for you. The good news is, I've come up with a way to take a car apart in seconds."

"Really?" Mac said dubiously.

"Really. The bad news is, it's a train."

■ ■ ■

"The good news," said the judge, "is that I find Mayor Knightly to be an honest politician.

"The bad news is, what I mean is that when he's bought off, he *stays* bought off."

■ ■ ■

"The other good news about the mayor," said the judge, "is that when he makes you a promise, he keeps it.

"The bad news is, he never makes promises."

■ ■ ■

Harry was tense, so he went to see his doctor. The next day his neighbor Gary saw him out in the yard.

"How'd it go yesterday?" Gary asked.

"There's good news and bad news. The good news is, the doctor said it would relax me to go outside and paint flowers.

"The bad news is, it's making me worse! The darn paint just won't stick to the petals!"

■ ■ ■

"I hear your daughter just graduated from the Food Institute," Mrs. Cullen said to Mrs. Erry. "I'll bet she's thrilled."

"To tell you the truth, there's good news and bad news about that.

"The good news is, she's already got a job.

The bad news is, it's at the insane asylum, where she's serving soup to nuts."

* * *

When T.J. came home from the pool hall, his mother asked, "Where's your brother Tony?"

"Ma," he said, "I got good news and bad news. Remember how you're always buggin' Tony about cleanin' his ears? The good news is, one of the guys did it for him."

"That's fine, but where is he?"

"The bad news is, he used a .45."

* * *

The woman was saying to her friend, "There's good news and bad news about my son having become President of the United States.

"The good news is, when we visit, we get to sleep in the White House.

"The bad news is, whenever we go out to dinner, he refuses to sign the bill."

* * *

"So," Sarah asked Jane, "how's married life?"

"It's good and bad. The good news is, my new husband has no hang-ups at all."

"You're lucky."

"Not really. The bad news is, I mean that when he takes off his clothes, he drops them on the floor."

■ ■ ■

Walking in after a hard day at the office, Murphy told his wife, "Good news! I found myself fired with enthusiasm today.

"The bad news is, I don't know *where* I'm going to find another job."

■ ■ ■

The inventor got a call from his financial backer.

"How's that new invention coming along?"

"Well, there's good news and bad news," said the inventor. "The good news is, I've invented a revolutionary new kind of burglar alarm."

"Good work! Bring it to the office."

"I can't. The bad news is, another inventor stole it."

■ ■ ■

The police were auctioning off all the goods they'd collected from a raid on the mob.

As a car was rolled in front of the audience, the auctioneer said, "The good news is, this car will cost you next to nothing.

"The bad news is, there's a hood in the front, one in the back, and another inside."

■ ■ ■

Wilson lost a fortune in the stock-market crash, and his accountant wanted to break it to him as easily as possible.

"Good news," the accountant said. "I just heard the latest dope from Wall Street.

"The bad news is, it's your investment counselor."

■ ■ ■

Mrs. Hill said to a friend, "The good news about my boy Harold is that he's not afraid of hard work.

"The bad news is, he's been fighting it for years."

■ ■ ■

Mrs. Dickerson said to her sister, "Good news! My husband won a weekend for two at a posh resort!

"The bad news is, he went twice."

■ ■ ■

Mrs. Dickerson added, "The good news was that when my husband got back, he promised we'd go out three times a week.

"The bad news is, he took Mondays, Thursdays, and Saturdays, and I get Tuesdays, Wednesdays, and Fridays."

■ ■ ■

Mrs. Dickerson concluded, "But there *is* good news: we've had twenty happy years of marriage.

"The bad news is, we've been married for forty years."

■ ■ ■

"Who says the people at the post office are illiterate?" the photographer said. "The good news is, I stamped a parcel 'Photos: Do Not Bend' and they read it, no problem.

"The bad news is, they wrote underneath it 'Oh Yes They Do!' "

■ ■ ■

The opera critic wrote, "The good news is that last night, during a performance of *Aïda*, I heard something amazing that I'd never heard before: the lead actually hit an amazing B above high C.

"The bad news is, she'd backed into a sword and had to sit out the rest of the performance."

■ ■ ■

It was the twenty-fifth anniversary of his publishing company, and owner Mr. Grumply came home from the office one day.

"Good news!" he told his wife. "All of the editors pitched in and bought us a paid vacation to Lake Ontario.

"The bad news is, it's a week on each of the Thousand Islands."

■ ■ ■

Actually, the good news about Mr. Grumply is that he's a hard worker who goes to every single editorial meeting. The bad news is, he listens to every idea put forth with an open mouth.

■ ■ ■

Talking to the pediatrician about her two-year-old, Mrs. Papa said, "There's good news and bad news about my daughter's progress.

"The good news is, I've taught her to look both ways before she crosses the street.

"The bad news is, she looks up and down."

■ ■ ■

After surviving the humongous flood, Morty met his friend Sherman.

"How'd you make out?" Sherman asked.

"There's bad news and good news. The bad news is, I lost almost everything I own."

"Almost?"

"Right. The good news is, I managed to save my lucky four-leaf clover."

SOME ROCK-AND-ROLL REVIEWS

"The good news," said the music critic, "is that the hot Rachlin Rollers gave a concert in Key Biscayne last night.

"The bad news is, it was the first time in their career that they knew what key they were in."

■ ■ ■

"The good news," said another music critic, "is that when I heard the rock-and-roll group, I couldn't stay in my seat.

"The bad news is, I was in the middle of the row and couldn't get out."

■ ■ ■

"The good news," wrote a third music critic, "is that the group had me clapping my hands in a minute.

"The bad news is, I mean over my ears."

"Doctor," Abraham said over the phone, "I'm calling from the next state, and I've got good news and bad news. The good news is, you've cured me of sleepwalking."

"I'm glad to hear that."

"The bad news is, now I sleep-hitchhike!"

■ ■ ■

Roy said to his friend Walt, "Y'know, there's good news and bad news where money is concerned.

"The good news is, making money is no problem. The bad news is, trying to pass it off as real is almost impossible!"

■ ■ ■

After returning from his vacation, Charlton said to Burt, "Good news! I left on the TV and all the lights in my apartment, and the place wasn't burglarized while I was away.

"The bad news is, I had a $3,000 electric bill."

■ ■ ■

Tired of having his car broken into, Jason had a special, customized vehicle built.

Meeting a friend at the mall, he said, "Yes—the good news is, this car is theftproof, break-in-proof, bullet-proof, and has self-inflating tires in case I get a flat.

"But there *is* bad news," he admitted as they walked to the parking lot.

"What's that?" asked the friend.

Jason said, "The bad news is, I locked my keys inside."

■ ■ ■

"Who says Los Angeles is too smoggy and dirty?" a native asked a New Yorker. "Why, the good news is, I opened my window just this morning and saw a bluebird sitting on my windowsill."

The New Yorker said, "The bad news is, it was a robin redbreast holding its breath."

■ ■ ■

"The good news," Jim told his friend, "is that I married my wife for her looks. The bad news is, I don't like the ones I get when I come home late."

■ ■ ■

"Good news," little Jennie said to her mother one morning, "I've invented pancakes that flip themselves over."

"Very nice, honey."

"The bad news is, how do you feel about pancakes with popcorn?"

■ ■ ■

"Who says American workers are lazy?" said the businesswoman. "Look at the post office. The good news is, I sent a letter from New York yesterday—and it got to Chicago the next day.

"The bad news is, I wanted it to go to Miami."

■ ■ ■

Upon reaching the airport, Ludwig was told by the ticket agent, "There's bad news and good news. The bad news is, you just missed the plane to Chicago.

"The good news is, you're *way* early for the next one."

■ ■ ■

Unlucky Luke was at Larry's house when he tripped and fell down the stairs, hit his head on a statue at the bottom, knocked it into a shelf, and caused it to fall on him.

When his wife came to visit him in the hospital, she said, "How're you feeling?"

"Well," said Luke, "there's good news and bad news. "The good news is, I got a very nice get-well card from Larry.

"The bad news is, when I opened it, I got a paper cut."

■ ■ ■

Arriving home, Terrence said to his wife, "I had some good news and bad news today.

"The good news is, while I was driving along Main Street, I swerved to avoid having a black cat cross in front of me."

"That's lucky!" she said. "What's the bad news?"

Terrence said, "The bad news is, when I swerved, I crashed into a mirror delivery truck."

■ ■ ■

Mr. Burke said to his friend, "You know, I'm really feeling the economic crunch. I've got two kids in college, and the bad news is the post office is raising rates again."

His friend said, "The good news is, postage will be so expensive, your kids won't be able to write home for money."

■ ■ ■

"The good news," one young musician said to another, "is that I often play for charity.

"The bad news is, I usually don't get it."

■ ■ ■

Penny said to her friend, "The good news is, I get along just fine with the girl next door. The bad news is, that's because we both love to fight."

■ ■ ■

The mega-rich Hollywood star told a friend, "The good news is that my marriage was made in heaven. The bad news is, all the particulars were worked out by very expensive lawyers."

■ ■ ■

Telling his children about the tough neighborhood he grew up in, Vance said, "The good news is, we had a terrific public transportation system.

"The bad news is, it was ambulances."

■ ■ ■

The TV anchor person came on the air and said, "Bad news, America: we've been invaded by Martians. But the good news is, they eat politicians and spit oil."

■ ■ ■

"Living in Los Angeles has its good points and bad points," George told his friend from New York. "The good news is, we have sunny weather all year round.

"The bad news is, who enjoys dreaming of a tan Christmas?"

* ■ *

The boy went over to his dad. "Pop, I just got a job—and there's good news and bad news.

"The good news is, I figured out how to save a *lot* of money.

"That bad news is, it's by using yours."

* ■ *

The producer told his financial backers, "The good news is, the movie was shot down by the coast in just ten days.

"The bad news is, it was shot down by the critics in just one day."

* ■ *

The producer added, "The good news is, one very influential critic said ours was a super movie. The bad news is, the critic meant that his apartment super could have done better."

* ■ *

After the Chinese gymnast returned home from a disappointing showing in the Olympics, one trainer said to another, "Good news! The government was not upset with Ling's execution.

"The bad news is, the rest of the team will miss her."

■ ■ ■

The aspiring author phoned the publisher to see how they'd liked his manuscript.

"I'm afraid I have some bad news for you," the editor told her. "We only publish books by authors with well-known names."

"That's *good* news!" she said. "*Everybody's* heard the name Smith!"

■ ■ ■

After walking through the tough neighborhood on his way home from school, Bennie burst into the kitchen.

"Good news, Ma! I made it through the Forbidden Zone and I *still* have all my teeth!

"The bad news is, ten of 'em are in my pocket."

■ ■ ■

"Good news!" Bruno said to his wife over the phone. "I'll be home early tonight 'cause I took public transportation.

"Da bad news is, if da cops call, tell 'em ya don't know nothin' about a missin' bus."

■ ■ ■

Little David arrived late for school again.

"Didn't I tell you to set an alarm clock?" the teacher scolded him.

"You did," David admitted, "and there's good news and bad news about that.

"The good news is, I set the clock for six and it went off.

"The bad news is, I'm the seventh member of the family!"

■ ■ ■

Lloyd asked his friend Clark, "How's that new secretary working out?"

"There's good news and bad news," said Clark. "The good news is, when I ask her to take a letter, she comes running. The bad news is, after she picks one from the mail basket, she leaves."

■ ■ ■

After being shown to his table in the out-of-the-way restaurant, the salesman rubbed his hands together and told the waiter, "Good news, my man! I'm hungry enough to eat a *horse!*"

The waiter whispered back, "Bad news, my man. You've come to the right place."

■ ■ ■

"The good news," said the widow, "is that my new beau is the salt of the earth. The bad news is, I can't seem to shake him."

■ ■ ■

Hardaway told the doctor, "Good news! I feel like a new man!"

"Bad news," the doctor replied. "The old one still owes me two hundred dollars."

■ ■ ■

"How was your date last night?" Derek asked his friend Hilton.

"There was good news and bad news. The good news was, I really impressed her by ordering the entire meal in Italian. The bad news was, we were in a Chinese restaurant."

■ ■ ■

"There's good news and bad news," the environmental specialist told her boss. "The bad news is, the water in the lake is thick with pollution.

"The good news is, if the dam ever bursts, at least the water'll stay put."

■ ■ ■

The teenager came home and told his father, "Good news, Dad! I just found out that the car really does stop on a dime.

"The bad news is, it was in the pocket of some guy who was crossing the street."

■ ■ ■

Arriving at the grocery store that had been the scene of a robbery, the police officer radioed the sergeant.

"The good news, sir, is that I arrived in time to nab one of them.

"The bad news is, it's the guy who was robbed."

■ ■ ■

Actually it wasn't the police officer's fault. The good news was, when he got there, he and his partner covered all the exits. The bad news was, the thief left by one of the entrances.

■ ■ ■

Talking about the opinionated movie star, the agent said, "The good news is, success hasn't gone to her head. The bad news is, it *has* gone to her mouth."

■ ■ ■

"There's good news and bad news about my new job," Morgan told his friend Jean.

"The bad news is, I'm only making five dollars an hour. The good news is, we're paid once a month so I don't get mad that often."

■ ■ ■

After scurrying up a large tree in Yosemite National Park, Harry said to Barry, "The good news is, the view from up here *is* spectacular.

"The bad news is, I don't think that bear plans to leave real soon. . . ."

■ ■ ■

The good news is, after years of trying, the senator finally was nominated for President and got his day in the sun.

The bad news is, he was sent back to the Senate with a bad case of sunburn.

■ ■ ■

"The good news," the mayor of the crime-ridden city said at a press conference, "is that our new foot patrol is working wonderfully. Robberies are way down."

"The bad news," shouted a reporter, "is that feet weren't what was being stolen."

■ ■ ■

The good news for the jailed gangster was that following week after week of confiding in his lawyer, his attorney finally got him off.

The bad news was that now the attorney knew too much. . . .

A POLITICAL TALE

"The good news," the reporter told her editor, "is that the mayor has been doing the work of two men.

"The bad news is, they're Frank and Jesse James."

■ ■ ■

"The bad news," the reporter went on, "is that the mayor has decided to run again.

"The good news is, it's for the town line."

■ ■ ■

"The good news," the reporter finished up, "is that if the mayor is reelected, he says he's going to get our city moving again.

"The bad news is, if he wins, I'm moving."

The doctor told his patient, a wealthy oilman, "I have good news and bad news. The good news is, we have a heart ready to transplant into your body. The bad news is, it came from a Democrat."

■ ■ ■

After seeing the new playwright's first play, the critic wrote, "There's good news and bad news.

"The good news is, this woman's a writer for the ages. The bad news is, it's ages five through eight."

■ ■ ■

The health official told the press, "The bad news is, the air over the coast will be thick with pollution all summer.

"The good news is, think of the money folks'll save on suntan lotion."

■ ■ ■

Jake kept getting fired.

"The good news," he said, "is that when I'm broke, I can always find a relative willing to help me out.

"The bad news is, I mean the door."

■ ■ ■

Pertwee told his friend, "Remember that ringing in my ears, the one that's been bothering me for years?"

"I sure do."

"The good news is, I've finally gotten rid of it. The bad news is, now I don't know when somebody's trying to call me."

■ ■ ■

"The good news," Mr. Tendler said to a friend, "is now that I have children, I know what true contentment is.

"The bad news is, it's gone forever."

■ ■ ■

"The good news," said the pollster to the president, "is that the editorial columnists have decided not to pick on you, because you haven't done anything.

"The bad news is, the people want to vote you out for the same reason."

■ ■ ■

Jolie came home after his first day at college.

"How did it go?" his mother asked.

"There's good news and bad news," Jolie said. "The good news is, the professor really knew what to talk about.

"The bad news is, it was about three hours."

■ ■ ■

After returning home from the doctor's office, Ira felt as sick as when he left. His wife asked why.

"There's good news and bad news," Ira said. "The good news is, Dr. Zarchy's been practicing medicine for thirteen years. The bad news is, in his case, practice hasn't made perfect."

■ ■ ■

"Good news!" the stockbroker shouted over the phone. "The market has broken 3750! The bad news is, I've got to call 3749 other clients and tell them they're also busted."

■ ■ ■

Explaining the U.S. political system to a bunch of students, the professor said, "There's good news and bad news about how the Senate operates.

"The good news is, they spend half their time passing laws that make this country a better place.

"The bad news is, they spend the other half of their time helping their friends get around those laws."

■ ■ ■

Hector and Harvey sat down in a restaurant.

"So," Hector asked, "do you come here a lot?"

"Yes, and there's good news and bad news about this place," Harvey said. "The good news is, the service is terrible."

"That's *good* news?" Hector said.

"Absolutely. Because the bad news is, the food is even worse."

■ ■ ■

"The good news," said Mrs. Mishnick, "is that my daughter just graduated from college and she's now a teacher.

"The bad news is, she's got no class."

■ ■ ■

The guard came running in to see the warden.

"Good news and bad news, sir. The good news is, prisoner 7271975 has married your daughter."

The warden rose from his chair, steam coming from his ears. "That's the *good* news, you fool? What could the bad news possibly be?"

"The bad news is, they eloped."

■ ■ ■

Describing her fiancé to her parents, Mary said, "The good news is, my husband-to-be takes orders from no one.

"The bad news is, he's the company's least successful salesperson."

* ■ *

After the aspiring comic returned from an audition at a comedy club, her roommate asked her how it went.

"There's good news and bad news," she said. "The good news was, I got the owner to laugh until tears ran down his face. The bad news is, it was when I said I wanted to be paid for performing."

* ■ *

Ugly Ursula came home from a blind date. "Good news," she said, phoning the mutual friend who had set it up. "Lum looked me over from head to toe and said I'm a perfect '10.' "

"Bad news," said her friend. "Lum's a shoe salesman."

* ■ *

"The good news," Diedre said about her fiancé, "is that he's the most eminent naval surgeon in the United States.

"The bad news," she said, "is we're both worried that maybe he's a little *too* specialized."

* ■ *

The heavy-metal singer called his manager. "How's my first recording doing?"

"There's good news and bad news," said the manager. "The good news is, sales are incredible. The bad news is, my friends sold theirs, my secretary sold hers, the critics sold theirs. . . ."

■ ■ ■

On his fiftieth anniversary, Hillyard took a long vacation. When he got back, his friends asked how it went.

"Good and bad," he said. "The good part about going around the world is that you get to see a little of so many different countries.

"The bad part about it is, next year my wife wants to go somewhere else."

■ ■ ■

"The good news," Rance said to his soon-to-be ex-boss, "is that you're really a swell guy. The bad news is, I mean around the head. . . ."

■ ■ ■

Mr. Petrie called Rob into the office.

"I have some good news and bad news, Rob," he said.

"Shoot."

"The good news is, I won't be doing that. The bad news is, you're fired."

■ ■ ■

Old Widow Brown went on a date. When she got back, her sister Mary asked how it was.

"There's good news and bad news," said the widow. "The good news was that we went to the movie and I had to slap him twice."

"A bit frisky, was he?"

"No," said the widow. "The bad news was that he fell asleep twice."

■ ■ ■

"The good news," Neal told his friend, "is that I was able to wire flowers for my mother-in-law on her birthday.

"The bad news is, she saw the TNT in time."

■ ■ ■

Old Mrs. Jenson asked her friend Mr. Olson how he enjoyed his date.

"The good news is, my date looked like a million bucks. The bad news is, she was all green and wrinkly."

■ ■ ■

"How was *your* blind date?" Mrs. Olson asked Mrs. Jenson.

"The good news," said Mrs. Jenson, "is that he was six-foot-two. The bad news is, I mean *around*."

■ ▦ ■

Two cannibals were having dinner.

"The bad news," said one, "is that I really can't stand the chief. The good news is, the rest of the meal is delicious."

■ ▦ ■

Bert told his friend, "The good news is, my car has *terrific* shocks.

"The bad news is, I mean it stops when you don't expect it, the brakes fail suddenly, the wipers don't work in the rain. . . ."

■ ▦ ■

The piano teacher came to see Mrs. Levitz after her son's lesson.

"The good news," said the teacher, "is that your boy plays just like Horowitz and Rubinstein.

"The bad news is, I mean he uses his fingers."

■ ▦ ■

"There's good news and bad news about the new fish market," Mrs. Lipson told her friend.

"The good news is, everything there is fresh. The bad news is, that includes the staff."

■ ■ ■

After a truly miserable winter, the local weathercaster came on TV and said, "I have good news and bad news.

"The good news is, I expect it to snow just once next week.

"The bad news is, it'll be for seven days."

■ ■ ■

Sarah Jane said to her friend, "The bad news is, I had to go for some X rays this morning.

"The good news is, the doctor saw something in me and asked me out."

■ ■ ■

Mrs. Forscht returned home from a shopping spree and asked her husband to help her unload the car.

"The good news," she told him, "was that I bought everything that was marked down.

"The bad news is, I haven't figured out *what* we're going to do with an escalator."

The art teacher came out to see Mrs. Dickerson when she came to pick up her daughter.

"I have good news and bad news," said the professor. "The good news is, your daughter paints better than Michelangelo and Raphael.

"The bad news is, I mean nowadays."

■ ■ ■

After buying a microwave oven, Marie told her neighbor, "The good news is, it really cooks food fast. The bad news is, my husband *hated* having Thanksgiving turkey at five in the morning."

■ ■ ■

Good news for rich people: money talks.
Bad news for the rest of us: money just goes without saying.

■ ■ ■

Telling a friend about his new bride, Chester said, "The good thing about her is, she's tough: she demands a man's pay. The bad news is, I wish it weren't mine."

■ ■ ■

Hardworking Mr. Cohen told a friend, "The good news is, I finally got to take my son to the zoo this weekend.

"The bad news is, they wouldn't keep him."

■ ■ ■

"The good news," wrote the TV critic, "is that thanks to cable, the pictures we get in our homes now are extremely clear.

"The bad news," she wrote, "is that most of the pictures we get in our homes now are extremely filthy."

■ ■ ■

The coach told the press, "As you know, we had some bad news today. Tackle Willie James was hurt and needed a transfusion.

"The good news is, the zoo was able to send a gorilla right over. . . ."

■ ■ ■

The Merritts rented a cabin in the woods, and while Ralph stayed in town to sign the papers, city girl Cindy drove over to tidy the place up.

Later, she came by to pick up her husband. "I've got good news," she said. "Everything's all clean, and I've got a big fire roaring in the den."

"I've got bad news," Ralph said. "There *is* no fireplace in the den."

■ ■ ■

Quincy got a job testing saddles at a factory. After a week his boss called him into her office.

"I've got good news and bad news, Quincy," she said. "The good news is, I like you a lot. The bad news is, I'm going to have to let you go for standing up on the job. . . ."

■ ■ ■

"I have good news and bad news," Allan told his wife. "The good news is that I finally traded in our old car."

"Wonderful!" she said. "What did you get for it?"

"That's the bad news," he said. "All I got was a ride home."

■ ■ ■

As his mother woke up from a long nap little Dickie ran up and tugged her sleeve.

"Mom, I have good news! While you were asleep a nice woman opened the door so Jakie could play with his ball and bat outside.

"The bad news is, the plane hadn't landed yet."

SOME BOXING
GOOD NEWS/BAD NEWS

The sportscaster was winding up his coverage of the boxing match.

"The good news for all you Kid Cody fans," he said, "is that the challenger came ready to *win*, getting out there and throwing a devastating left-right-left combination.

"The bad news is, then the champ got into the ring and murdered him."

■ ■ ■

The next week the sportscaster called another fight.

"The good news," he said, "is that the champ is completely covered with blood.

"The bad news is, it's the challenger's."

■ ■ ■

The following week the sportscaster finished up his coverage of yet another fight.

"The good news," he said, "is that the challenger has the most spectacular rabbit punch I've ever seen.

"The bad news is, they're making him fight people."

■ ■ ■

Covering his fourth and final fight, the sportscaster said, "The good news is, the challenger hit the champ with three quick blows.

"The bad news is, after the champ's fourth punch, the challenger couldn't draw another breath."

■ ■ ■

When George came home, he found his new bride hysterical and a neighbor trying to console her.

"What's wrong?" he asked.

"I have bad news and good news," the neighbor said. "The bad news is, your dog ate the stew she was cooking for dinner."

"That's not so terrible. What's the good news?"

"The good news," she went on, "is that the pet store has promised to find the same kind of dog right away."

■ ■ ■

John walked into the apartment with his violin.

"Where have you been?" his wife, Beryl, demanded.

"You've always scoffed at my talent," he said, "but I have good news! I, John Taylor, have just played the violin at Carnegie Hall!

"The bad news is, the police chased me away before a crowd could gather."

■ ■ ■

Norman had the same kind of luck.

"Honey," he said bursting into his apartment, "boy, do I have good news! I've been signed to play in Yankee Stadium!

"But I also have bad news: organists only make five bucks an hour."

■ ■ ■

After building a playground for his kids, Maurice got some bad news from the tots: he had built the slide with much too little slope.

The good news is, after studying the problem, he found he had the inclination to fix it.

■ ■ ■

Then there was the case of Jack Redmond. The good news is, he was permitted to settle all his debts with a charge.

The bad news was, the charge was in an electric chair.

■ ■ ■

Six-year-old Rudy had a reputation for being a little lady's man, and when five-year-old Sarah went to play with him, her mother wasn't thrilled.

When Sarah came home, her mother asked how her day was.

"Oh, it was good and bad."

"What was the good part?" her mother asked.

Sarah said, "The good part was when he said we should hold hands."

Her mother's eyes went wide. "And what was the bad part?"

"When he cheated and kept dealing himself all the good cards," Sarah replied.

■ ■ ■

The good news is, the President finally decided to tour the big cities, starting with Detroit, and asked Air Force One to fly him to where all the cars are made.

The bad news is, he ended up in Tokyo.

■ ■ ■

The boss addressed his staff.

"The bad news is, because of the recession, we're all going to have to stay an hour later to bring in more business.

"The good news is, there's nothing that

boosts morale better than an occasional change of close."

■ ■ ■

"The good news," said the heavyset woman, "is that all of my weight is just water weight.

"The bad news is, it's the Atlantic Ocean."

■ ■ ■

When millionaire Hulbert Dingleberry died, his son Danton went to see their lawyer.

"What does the will say?" Danton asked. "Did Dad remember me?"

"There's good news and bad news. The good news is, yes, your father remembered you in his will."

"Great! Hot dog! I'm set for life!"

"The bad news is, all it says, 'Hi, Danton. Guess who's going to have to get a job?' "

■ ■ ■

When Danton still didn't get it, the lawyer put it another way.

"I have good news and bad news. The good news is, you've inherited a fortune.

"The bad news is, it begins with *mis*."

■ ■ ■

The judge tried to break the verdict easily to Mr. Ripper.

"I have good news and bad news," she said. "The good news is, I'm going to make you pretty as a picture.

"The bad news is, you're going to hang."

■ ■ ■

The pollster phoned Mr. Strickhartz. "What do you think of the presidential candidate?" he asked.

"Well, there's good news and bad news," said Strickhartz. "The good news is, thanks to his ads, I think more and more about him.

"The bad news is, thanks to his ads, I think less and less of him."

■ ■ ■

"The good news," the accountant said to his client, "is that your ship has finally come in.

"The bad news is, the government's going to be there unloading it."

■ ■ ■

"There's good news and bad news about my new boss Vance," Wally told a friend.

"The good news is, he's the absolute best at what he does.

"The bad news is, what he does is brag."

■ ■ ■

Not that Wally was much of a prize. When Vance had lunch with the owner of the company, he told her, "You know Wally Smith? Well, there's good news and bad news about him.

"The good news is, he really does want to work in the worst way.

"The bad news is, that's *exactly* how he works."

■ ■ ■

"The good news," the psychologist told the audience at the old-age home, "is that you're only as old as you think."

"The bad news," shouted a jaded listener, "is that that makes you about three and a half."

■ ■ ■

Mike had had it with the city, and bought a home in the woods.

"The good news," he told his wife, Penny, "is that we can take our baths in the spring."

"And the bad news," said Penny, "is that we'll smell for the other three seasons."

■ ■ ■

"The good news," the accountant told his client, "is that the Internal Revenue Service has a new payment plan for people in your situation—you pay them nothing a month."

"Nothing? *Really?*"

"Right. The bad news is, you pay one hundred percent down."

■ ■ ■

A music critic had even less praise for an aspiring opera star.

"The good news," wrote the critic, "is that Roberto has a great voice.

"The bad news is, not for a human being."

■ ■ ■

The newlywed told her sister, "The good news is, my Hank is *just* what the doctor ordered.

"The bad news is, he's a pill."

■ ■ ■

"The good news about Myra," said one catty girl to another, "is that she has everything a boy could possibly want.

"The bad news is, I mean muscles and a beard."

■ ■ ■

The bad news is, *The First Good News/ Bad News Joke Book* is over.

The good news is, *The Second Good News/ Bad News Joke Book* is on the way!

■ ■ ■

RIB-TICKLING BOOKS

☐ **THE UNOFFICIAL DENTIST'S HANDBOOK by Candy Schulman with illustrations by Ian Ross.** More laughs than nitrous-oxide—this hilarious book, brimming with outrageous illustrations, makes an ideal gift for every practitioner and every patient who has trouble understanding what's so funny about oral surgery. (265959—$7.95)

☐ **THE UNOFFICIAL MOTHER'S HANDBOOK by Norma and Art Peterson.** The essential guide for the only person who ever applauded when you went to the bathroom; the adjudicator of who hit whom first; the person known to begin sentences with "You'll be sorry when . . ." Here is an affectionately funny survey of motherhood from "day 1" through "leaving the nest" and "are you back again?" (262461—$6.95)

☐ **THE JOYS OF YINGLISH by Leo Rosten.** "What a book! A celebration of scholarship, humor and linguistic anthropology." —William F. Buckley, Jr. "Open it anywhere for a laugh. Or start with *abracadabra* and work through *zlob* for an education and endless amusement."—*Booklist* (265436—$14.95)

Prices slightly higher in Canada.

Buy them at your local bookstore or use this convenient coupon for ordering.

NEW AMERICAN LIBRARY
P.O. Box 999 – Dept. #17109
Bergenfield, New Jersey 07621

Please send me the books I have checked above.
I am enclosing $_____ (please add $2.00 to cover postage and handling).
Send check or money order (no cash or C.O.D.'s) or charge by Mastercard or VISA (with a $15.00 minimum). Prices and numbers are subject to change without notice.

Card #_____ Exp. Date _____
Signature_____
Name_____
Address_____
City _____ State _____ Zip Code _____

For faster service when ordering by credit card call **1-800-253-6476**

Allow a minimum of 4-6 weeks for delivery. This offer is subject to change without notice.

RIB TICKLERS!
by Jeff Rovin

☐ **1001 GREAT SPORTS JOKES.** From football and basketball to bodybuilding, boxing, the rodeo, tennis, golf and every other sport—here are the funniest jokes ever to touch base and score in the great game of laughter! (169654—$4.99)

☐ **1,001 GREAT JOKES.** Over 1,000 jokes, one-liners, riddles, quips and puns—for every audience and every occasion. Among the topics skewered in this collection are: bathrooms, yuppies, hillbillies, sex, small towns, weddings, writers and much more! (168291—$4.95)

☐ **1,001 MORE GREAT JOKES.** Once again we've set a new standard in the wittiest, wackiest, most outrageous in adult humor. Here are jokes for every occasion—from raising chuckles from friends and family, to rousing roars of laughter from all kinds of audiences. Even better, the jokes are organized alphabetically by subject—so open up this book for a nonstop feast of fun from A to Z. (159799—$4.99)

☐ **1,001 GREAT ONE-LINERS.** The greatest one-line jokes, observations, and commentaries, for the first time, put together as a source of information and inspiration for anyone who wants to brighten up a conversation, a speech, or a piece of writing. Instantly prepare and swiftly serve up a feast of laughter. (164229—$3.99)

☐ **1,001 GREAT PET JOKES.** Laughter is raining down cats and dogs! (172612—$3.99)

Prices slightly higher in Canada

Buy them at your local bookstore or use this convenient coupon for ordering.

NEW AMERICAN LIBRARY
P.O. Box 999 – Dept. #17109
Bergenfield, New Jersey 07621

Please send me the books I have checked above.
I am enclosing $_____ (please add $2.00 to cover postage and handling). Send check or money order (no cash or C.O.D.'s) or charge by Mastercard or VISA (with a $15.00 minimum). Prices and numbers are subject to change without notice.

Card #_____ Exp. Date _____
Signature_____
Name_____
Address_____
City _____ State _____ Zip Code _____

For faster service when ordering by credit card call **1-800-253-6476**

Allow a minimum of 4-6 weeks for delivery. This offer is subject to change without notice.